Business-to-Business Prospecting

Innovative Techniques to Get Your Foot In the Door with Any Prospect

Andrea Sittig-Rolf

Published by Aspatore, Inc.

For corrections, company/title updates, comments or any other inquiries, please e-mail info@aspatore.com.

First Printing, 2005

10 9 8 7 6 5 4 3 2 1

ISBN 1-59622-205-0 Library of Congress Control Number: 2005927746

Managing Editor, Leah M. Jones, Edited by Michaela Falls, Cover Design by Emily Shirley

Material in this book is for educational purposes only. This book is sold with the understanding that neither the author nor the publisher is engaged in rendering medical, legal, accounting, investment, or any other professional advice or service in connection with this book. For legal advice, please consult your personal lawyer.

This book is printed on acid free paper.

The views expressed by the individuals in this book do not necessarily reflect the views shared by the companies they are employed by (or the companies mentioned in this book).

The headshot photo on the cover of the book was taken by Rex Tranter.

Happy Prospecting
Becky!

:)

[signature]

Table of Contents

Acknowledgments

The purpose of writing this book is to give readers insight into the ways to effectively prospect for new business-to-business clients, and ultimately, close more sales. Because this book is a compilation of years of experience as a sales professional, sales manager, entrepreneur, and business owner, I want to acknowledge and thank several people who supported and influenced me along the way.

Bob Powers, my first sales manager, thanks for seeing in me what I did not yet see in myself. Our first meeting at the Honey Bear Bakery was the reason I chose sales as a career.

Doug and Kay Bickerstaff, the best people you could ever hope to work with, and even better people to have as friends. Thanks for believing in me and always supporting my career choices.

Keith Cupp, a great manager and friend who taught me about professionalism and ethics in the world of sales. Thanks for your leadership.

My parents, may they rest in peace. Thanks for your unconditional love and support over the years. I miss you both.

My older siblings, Katy, Janet, and Carl; thanks for your guidance and encouragement.

And of course, I especially want to thank my husband, Brian, for encouraging me to be all I can be. Thanks for your love, support, and confidence in me. I love you very much!

Introduction

If there is one thing you could improve upon regarding your role as a sales professional, what would it be? Find more opportunities? Close more deals? Make more money? Based on my own experience as a sales professional of more than fifteen years, I would estimate that what you care about most is the end result of your sales activity—the close. Funny thing is that the very first phase of the sales process—the prospecting phase—often has the most impact on the last phase of the sales process, the closing phase. Therefore, when analyzing your sales pipeline, you will find a direct correlation between the quality of your prospects and the quantity of your sales.

Think of your best customer. How did the relationship start? What did you do to get the appointment, gain their trust, and close the sale? Throughout the process of working with this customer, did they return your calls, respond to your e-mails, and call you with questions? My guess is yes. Why? What did you do to earn this level of respect from your customer when they were still a prospect? Did you have to ask for the sale? My guess is no. The point is that when you take the time to effectively prospect for new business, to qualify leads, and to build trust with your prospects, the "close" is not something you have to ask for, but rather something that happens naturally because you used effective prospecting techniques right from the beginning.

For those of you who have chosen to read this book simply because you would like more ideas on how to get your foot in the door with new prospects, you have chosen wisely. For those of you who want more information on how to close more sales, keep reading, you too have chosen wisely.

Rest assured that this book does not cover the same old prospecting techniques you will find in every other sales book on the market. Quite the contrary—here you will learn innovative business-to-business prospecting techniques such as creating your Ideal Client Profile and cleaning up the pipeline to focus on real opportunities. From generating qualified leads through free online resources to networking with colleagues by giving leads first, this book will explain step-by-step how you can become an exceptional prospector. Other unique ideas include contacting keynote speakers before an event to receive a form of free advertising with your core audience. Also, you will get great advice on how to win ambassadors among prospects who will sell for you when you are not there. Furthermore, you will learn how to plan and facilitate powerful workshops that allow you to present to multiple prospects at one time. You will also discover how to build valuable strategic alliances to "sell smarter" by empowering someone else to do the prospecting for you. Finally, this book will explain how to write compelling case studies so you will understand how to leverage your existing customers in order to win new customers.

This book not only outlines a series of effective business-to-business prospecting techniques, but also includes activities that will help you generate more opportunities, create trust and credibility with prospects, and ultimately close more business with the kind of clients who are best suited for your product or service.

I encourage you to read the book once in its entirety and then go back and read it again, completing each of the activities presented at the end of each chapter. When you have finished doing that, you will have created a portfolio of powerful new business-to-business prospecting tools that will dramatically improve your sales results and overall income level.

I would love to hear about your results using the prospecting techniques offered in this book. Please e-mail me at contactus@sittignw.com or call 206-769-4886.

Happy prospecting!

Andrea Sittig-Rolf
Redmond, Washington

Part One: Knowing Your Ideal Client
Cleaning Up the Pipeline and Focusing on Real Opportunities

1

Defining the ICP (Ideal Client Profile)

"I don't know the key to success, but the key to failure is trying to please everybody."
Bill Cosby

Have you ever had clients who were more trouble than they were worth? Oftentimes we're so anxious to close the deal that we don't think about whether we really want that particular client or not. My guess is, however, that for the clients who turn out to be more trouble than they're worth, you had some inkling or gut feeling about them right from the beginning of the sales process. You had intuition that it might be a "high maintenance" client or worse, a "nightmare client," but for whatever reason, you didn't pay attention to your inner voice. The fact is, we're better off saying no to an opportunity than taking it based on the hardship and energy drain it may cost us in the long run.

The financial services industry has figured out that creating an Ideal Client Profile is the key to success in their business, and I think we should all follow their lead. Not only do financial advisors use the Ideal Client Profile as a tool to help them determine their best clients, they use it as a tool to help their prospects determine that they might, in fact, be an ideal client for the financial advisor. The financial advisor's Ideal Client Profile is even worded in such a way that anyone reading it would like to think of themselves as an ideal client for that financial advisor. In other words, the stated Ideal Client Profile is appealing to prospective clients because it uses flattering terminology. Below is an excerpt of one financial services company's Ideal Client Profile that I found on the Internet:

At Canterbury Financial Group, we serve successful individuals who expect excellence and have made a firm commitment to achieving it themselves. In general, the people who benefit most from our services tend to fit the following description:

> *Recognize the connection between accumulated assets and the freedom to pursue their life vision*
> *Successful in their careers*
> *Respected in the community*
> *Involved in rewarding activities or still employed*
> *Friendly, helpful, open-minded*
> *Consider managing money a burden, not a hobby*

Our Clients:

- Share in the realization that the freedom to pursue their compelling life vision is linked to their accumulated assets
- Want to simplify their lives and are willing to enter into a mutually beneficial long-term relationship with a personal wealth manager
- Are highly motivated to work with a fee-only adviser who knows them personally and has only their best interests in mind
  Canterbury Financial Group Ideal Client Profile found online at http://www.canterburygroup.com/idealclient/

I don't know about you, but after reading this company's Ideal Client Profile, it makes me want to sign up! So, not only does the Ideal Client Profile serve as a tool for you to target your prospecting activities, it can also serve as a marketing tool to your prospects who will want to be considered your Ideal Client.

Imagine if you had such a tool for your prospects to use to then tell you that they would like to be your next ideal client. How powerful would such a tool be to leverage in your marketing materials and prospecting activities?

In this chapter, I will cover how to create your Ideal Client Profile and then use it as a powerful business-to-business prospecting tool.

How many times have you actually thought about who your ideal client is, versus finding the next person who you think is just willing to buy from you? Think about it. Think about how your business would change if it was made up of "ideal clients." Think about an ideal client you currently work with. What makes them ideal? What are the parameters of, or formula for, your ideal client? What size company are they? How many employees do they have? How much do they do in revenue each year? Who are their clients? What is their product or service? How many locations do they have? How do they go to market (i.e. direct vs. indirect sales, retail, channel sales, etc.)? How much revenue do you do each year with your ideal client? Do you do repeat business with your ideal client? How many decision makers must you deal with to get a "yes" in working with your ideal client? How much client service is involved in working with your ideal client? Does your ideal client give you referrals to other ideal clients? These are all questions that should be considered when defining your ideal client profile (hereinafter referred to as "ICP") that will also lead to certain industries or specific vertical markets, who will make excellent prospects for you based on the nature of their industry or business, as identified in your ICP.

In defining your ICP, you can begin to focus only on those clients who fit your ICP. This also allows you to quickly identify someone who is *not* an ideal client and move on to someone who is. Think about how much more effective you could be in attracting ideal clients when you're no longer wasting time with prospects who aren't the best fit for what you sell anyway, for whatever reason. It took me two years after starting my business to realize the difference between ideal clients and non-ideal clients. Because we offer many different sales training and consulting programs, for purposes of this chapter I will focus on our sales training program called "The Blitz Experience™." The Blitz Experience™ is an activity-based sales training program that helps salespeople become more effective when prospecting over the phone. It is unique because it requires the salespeople to actually *practice* what they learn during the training on *real prospects*, resulting in a pipeline full of new opportunities at the end of the training.

When I started the company, I initially focused on any company, no matter what size, that had a sales team of at least three people. Without knowing it, that is how I was defining my ICP: companies who had a sales team of at least three people. That's it—no other factors were taken into consideration. This approach forced me to "start over" not only each month, but literally each day to determine where my next paycheck was coming from, since there was often no potential for any future business with that client. And believe me, that's no way to live! I was successful at finding clients, but running myself ragged because they were mostly small, one Blitz Experience™ opportunity clients.

Two years after starting my business, I stumbled onto an account that had a large sales team in the form of a "dealer network." It was a commercial furniture manufacturing company who went to market not through a direct sales channel, but through manufacture rep companies and dealers across the country who sold their products to the end user. Lo and behold, I had hit the mother lode and didn't even know it! It started small, with a Blitz Experience™ program here and there, but soon word got out and I had to actually hire other "Blitz Masters™" (sales trainers), just to meet the demand that was created for the Blitz Experience™ program within their dealer network! The next client I landed had a similar profile except that they were a major software manufacturing company. They too went to market not through a direct sales channel, but through a dealer network as well. Similar to the commercial furnishings company, this client began with two Blitz Experience™ programs with a dealer in North Carolina and when the program was so successful at that location, I received an e-mail from the general manager telling me he wanted to roll out the program to the remaining 300 sales reps in eight other cities! That single project generated more revenue for my company than all of the revenue my company had generated in the previous two years combined! Finally, after two years, I had begun to get the hang of it. I got to thinking, hmmm, what IS it about these two clients that is so different from the other clients I'd been working with? That's when I decided to create a formal process to determine my ICP. First, by defining the ideal client, and then pursuing only those prospects that fit the ICP, I would have an entire business focused on only the best of the best. I would also learn to quickly identify who fit the ICP and who did not so that I could move on quickly in situations where a prospect was not ideal according to the profile. I thought, why not turn the tables on this whole sales game? Why does it have to be that the client gets to choose whether or not to work with my company; why can't I choose which clients I want to work with? Once I began following this newfound methodology, my average order went from $2,000 in revenue to $17,000 in revenue! I actually increased my revenue by eight and a half times my average just by deciding what it was about these two new accounts that made them so lucrative for my business. Yes, I know, the suspense is killing you, so here it is—The Blitz Experience™ ICP:

Sittig Northwest, Inc.'s Ideal Client Profile

Client must have multiple locations.
Client must have a minimum of fifty sales reps.
Client must have a minimal number of decision makers.
Client must be willing and able to pay on Sittig Northwest's terms.
Client must be willing and able to "sell" The Blitz Experience™ within their organization.

Client must be willing and able to work with Sittig Northwest regarding program preparation details of the Blitz Experience™ program in order to ensure its success.

The point in using the ICP as a powerful prospecting tool is not to eliminate otherwise *good* prospects from your pipeline, but to eliminate prospects who are not "playing ball" with you and who meet less than about 70 percent of your ICP. The ICP is meant to be a guide not only to find new prospects, but also to help gauge the likelihood of turning a particular prospect in your *current pipeline* into a customer. It may be that you have prospects in your pipeline that meet 70 percent of your ICP, they are easy to work with, and have a genuine interest in your products and services. Prospects meeting those criteria, you may decide, are worth pursuing.

Another key element in creating your ICP is that it can also be used to help identify and qualify vertical markets. For example, when developing The Blitz Experience™ ICP it became obvious that manufacturing companies who go to market via dealer networks or channel partners are ideal client prospects of The Blitz Experience™ sales training program.

Manufacturing companies quickly see the value of offering professional sales training to their channel partners while requiring their channel partners to focus on promoting the manufacturing company's products during the training. For manufacturing companies, using The Blitz Experience™ sales training program in this way creates a win-win for both the manufacturing company and its dealers and channel partners. Therefore, a vertical market for The Blitz Experience™ is manufacturing companies who go to market using dealers and channel partners to sell their products.

Furthermore, creating your ICP will also help you identify and qualify channel partners and strategic alliances for your products and services. A channel partner is defined as a company who targets the same prospects you do, and who has the ability to present your products and services to their customers. A channel partner, once trained on your products and service, can become an invaluable source of distribution at a level that you as an individual could never accomplish.

Finally, creating your ICP will also help you identify and qualify strategic alliances. A strategic alliance, as is defined later in this book in chapter sixteen, is the science or art of sales tactics applied to the overall planning and conduct of large-scale business operations agreed to between companies with a common cause. So, for example, my company, Sittig Northwest, Inc. has a strategic alliance with several marketing companies who include The Blitz Experience™ sales training program as a tactic in the overall marketing strategy that they present to their clients. By leveraging my strategic alliance partners in the hunt for new business, I reduce the amount of time I must spend in finding new prospects. In other words, my strategic alliance partners are, in effect, doing the prospecting for me and bringing me in the loop once they've sold their client on the idea of a Blitz Experience™ program as a tactic to be included in their overall strategic plan.

2

Knowing Why Each Element of the ICP is Important

fter defining my ICP, it was important to know why each of the elements I listed as a part of the ICP was important. Here is the breakdown for Sittig Northwest's ICP:

Client must have multiple locations.

Important because multiple locations mean multiple opportunities.

Client must have a minimum of fifty sales reps.

Important because this represents a certain number of Blitz Experience™ programs that will generate a minimum amount of revenue worth pursuing.

Client must have a minimum number of decision makers.

Important because the fewer people who are involved in the decision making process, the less effort required by Sittig Northwest to sell The Blitz Experience™ program.

Client must be willing and able to pay on Sittig Northwest's terms.

Important because of cash flow control and expense incurred as a result of delivering The Blitz Experience™ program to the client.

Client must be willing and able to sell The Blitz Experience™ program within their organization.

Important because a minimum effort is required by Sittig Northwest to continue to sell to an existing client and as the lead trainer, I am more available for the training piece of the program, rather than the selling piece.

Client must be willing and able to work with Sittig Northwest regarding program preparation details of the Blitz Experience™ program in order to ensure its success.

Important because the client has certain responsibilities regarding the success of The Blitz Experience™ program implementation.

What came next, after defining my ICP, was the realization that by nature of certain industries, there was an automatic fit with my ICP. For example, I soon realized that commercial office furniture and software manufacturing companies were both excellent vertical markets because of the way they went to market through dealer networks, indicating that the same type of opportunity existed because of these particular industries and the way they traditionally go to market. After selecting other commercial office furniture and software manufacturing companies, the only other determining factor was their size. If they were a small manufacturing company and only had a handful of dealers, it was not something I would pursue; however, if they were a large company with an extensive dealer network, then it was something I would pursue.

3

Creating Your Ideal Client Survey

A nother important element in creating your ICP is to include your ideal clients in the process. For example, create a survey that your ideal clients can complete online and offer them an incentive for doing so. By soliciting help from your clients, you can gather crucial information from them as to exactly why they chose to do business with you and your company versus your competition. You may think you know why your clients buy from you, but until you ask them, you may be making false assumptions or missing solid selling points of your product or service that your clients see as valuable but you have neglected to include in your pitch to new prospects. Let me give you an example of what I mean. Take a look at my ideal client survey and begin thinking about how you might apply it to your business. Next to each survey question, I will also include why it is important to know the answer to the question from your client's point-of-view.

Sittig Northwest, Inc. Blitz Experience™ Ideal Client Survey

Why did you choose to do business with Sittig Northwest, Inc.?

Start with the most important question first, which is the "why" question. If your ideal clients answer no other survey questions, you will still have some good information about why they chose to do business with you and your company, which is the single most important piece of information you need to know when creating your Ideal Client Profile.

What criteria did you consider when making your decision? (i.e. price, value of training, timing of sales training offering filled an immediate need in your company, etc.)?

This question speaks to the decision making criteria and process that your ideal clients consider when making buying decisions regarding your products and services. The better feel you have for this information, the more specific you can be in your prospecting approach to immediately hit your prospects' hot buttons and grab their attention.

Which of our competitors did you consider when making your decision?

Hearing from your ideal clients who or what else they considered when making their buying decision is invaluable in understanding who your perceived competitors are and what other scenarios you may be up against in the sales process. Keep in mind that your client's perception is their reality. For example, my sales training program is often compared to hiring another full-time sales rep, and not necessarily another sales training program. If this is the case, I need to effectively communicate to my prospects that by making their existing sales team more effective, they will eliminate the need to add headcount, thus saving them quite a bit of money in the long run. If my sales training program is being compared to other sales training programs and the ideal client chose us, I need to know that too, again, in order to effectively communicate to prospects why my customers choose us over other sales training offerings.

Why did you not choose one of them instead of us?

The answer to this question will give you insight as to the perceived weaknesses of your competitors from your ideal client's perspective. A key selling technique is to compare your company's strengths to your competitor's weaknesses. Leverage the answer to this question to give you the ammunition you need to sell against your competitors.

Before choosing to do business with us, were you looking for our specific type of sales training or did we contact you first?

By understanding the answer to this question, you will better understand the most effective way to prospect for your ideal clients by having them tell you. For example, if most of your ideal clients tell you they were looking specifically for your type of products and services, and you just happened to be there, then you know that timing is everything and you need to base your prospecting efforts on making sure you're at the right place at the right time with your prospects, which usually requires "doing the numbers" and contacting many prospects until you hit the ones that have the perfect situation for your products and services. However, if your ideal clients tell you that you contacted them first, you will know that it's up to you to create the need for your products and services within your ideal clients and prospects.

How long did it take you to make your decision regarding our sales training once we presented our offering?

Knowing the sales cycle for your products and services is key in helping you determine your prospecting activity so that your pipeline is full of opportunities at all times to maintain consistency in your sales results.

What events, if any, triggered your decision to move forward with our offering (i.e. recent downturn in sales, new sales force, event promotion, new products and services promotion)?

If you understand the "trigger events" for your ideal clients, then you'll know what to look for in your prospects. So, for example, if you sell commercial office furniture, a trigger event may be when a company is moving. Chances are, if they're moving, they're going to need new office furniture.

How did you initially hear of us?

The answer to this question offers valuable information as to whether your ideal clients come from cold calls, referrals, personal introductions or a combination of all of the above. This information will help insure your prospecting activities are in line with how your ideal clients prefer to be approached.

When considering choosing us as a vendor, did you have a budget for sales training or did you need to find budget for it once you determined sales training was necessary?

The answers to budgetary questions are important to understand because they speak to whether prospects typically have a budget already outlined for your products and services or if you have the option of being creative with budgetary issues. For example, sometimes in my business, prospects don't have a budget specifically for sales training; however, they may have a marketing budget to tap into. If you are able to hone your skills in matters of budget with the prospects who fit your ICP, you will increase your sales results significantly.

Remember that this is not a client satisfaction survey. You may find yourself wanting to include questions such as, "Are you happy with your decision in choosing us?" or "Did you find our process in bringing you on as a client favorable?" or "Will you choose us again when faced with the same opportunity?" The ideal client survey is not to determine client satisfaction, but to determine who your ideal clients are and what they look like in terms of industry, employee size, annual revenue, and so on. You can feel free to do a separate survey to gain information about client satisfaction, but don't do it as a part of the ideal client survey. Also, note that the questions in the survey are all open-ended and start with words like what, when, why, where, and how. Asking open-ended questions will encourage your clients to answer the question in detail and in their own words. Try to avoid posing yes/no questions that limit the amount of information you will be able to gather from your ideal clients.

Once you have defined your ICP, you know why each of the elements you've included is important, and you have solicited feedback from your ideal clients via an ideal client survey, you should now begin to pursue only those prospects that fit your ICP. Also consider how your ICP might indicate certain vertical markets or specific industries you will pursue. A good way to determine industry-specific ideal clients or certain ideal vertical markets is to first consider one of your best clients, and then look at their competitors. The logic here is that by working with a particular client in the given industry or vertical market, you have already shown your product or service to be of benefit to this particular industry or vertical market. In looking at an ideal client's competition, you have many new prospects to pursue with proven benefits and results to get your foot in the door.

By using your ICP as a guide each time you generate a lead, you will begin to fill your pipeline with only those opportunities that are ideal in terms of your business and its growth, as well as determine the most likely clients who will be optimally satisfied with what you have to offer. You will also determine quickly those prospects that do *not* fit your ICP and move on to others who do, allowing you to focus on the very best opportunities possible for your business. It can be a challenge to say no to any business, even "bad" business sometimes, because we feel pressured to meet quotas and income goals, but don't be tempted just because someone appears to have an interest in what you sell. Oftentimes closing "bad business" can be much worse than saying no to "bad business." Remember, it is up to YOU to *choose your clients* based on your ICP, and the more you are willing to say no to the wrong type of clients, the more available you'll be to find and work with the right clients!

ACTIVITY PART ONE: Define Your ICP

ACTIVITY PART TWO: Define Why Each Element of Your ICP is Important

Create your own ICP by completing the questions below based on the specific criteria that make up your ideal client as well as explain *why* the answers to these questions are important to define. (Review this chapter using my example as a guide.)

What size company is my ideal client?

Why is this important?

What industry or industries does my ideal client represent?

Why is this important?

How many employees do they have?

Why is this important?

How much money do they generate in revenue each year?

Why is this important?

Who are their clients?

Why is this important?

What is their product or service?

Why is this important?

How many locations do they have?

Why is this important?

How do they go to market (i.e. direct vs. indirect sales, retail, channel sales, etc.)?

Why is this important?

How much revenue do I do each year with my ideal client?

Why is this important?

Do I do repeat business with my ideal client?

Why is this important?

How many decision makers must I deal with to get a "yes" in working with my ideal client?

Why is this important?

How much client service is involved from me personally in working with my ideal client?

Why is this important?

Does my ideal client give me referrals to other ideal clients?

Why is this important?

Use the space below to list other questions and answers that are important in defining your ICP.

ACTIVITY PART THREE: Create your Ideal Client Survey using the Sittig Northwest, Inc. Blitz Experience™ Survey as a guide

4

Discovering That Good Luck is When Opportunity Meets Preparedness

"I'm a great believer in luck, and I find the harder I work the more I have of it."
Thomas Jefferson

"As we become aware of our feelings and emotions and cause through imaging new representations in alignment with the feelings and emotions we desire, we alter the course, we see new scenery, we cultivate new contacts, create new communities and begin new lives…"
John Felitto

I love the saying by Napoleon Hill—"Good luck is when opportunity meets preparedness." Isn't that great? What I love about it is that it gives personal power to the word *luck*. In other words, the word *luck* indicates we have no control or power over the good things that happen to us. In contrast, this new suggestion for the meaning of the word *luck* gives us personal control and the ability to be lucky. Think about it. If you continue to grow as a person by staying healthy, keeping up-to-date with current events, continuing education in your career, and so on, when opportunity arises you not only recognize it as opportunity, but are prepared to work the opportunity as it satisfies your own goals of personal fulfillment. Consider your work as a sales professional. In promoting your business or product to your prospects, you are preparing yourself for an opportunity you hope to discover in your prospecting efforts. If you are ill-prepared when the opportunity presents itself or if you continue to prepare yourself for opportunity, but don't find it, you may be considered *unlucky*. However, when you prepare yourself for an opportunity and find it, you become *lucky*. When you think about it, it's an insult when you are successful and people call you *lucky* because it diminishes the fact that you worked hard for your success and that it wasn't just *dumb luck*!

One suggestion I have on becoming *lucky* is to first be very clear on what it is that makes you happy. Whether in your personal or professional life, put your energy towards the things that make you happy, then set the stage or build the foundation for fulfillment. I'm always amazed when I hear people talking about the things they want, yet behaving in a way that brings the complete opposite result! For instance, I have a friend who when she was single always talked about marrying someone who was about her age, who had never been married, and who didn't already have kids, but who wanted to have kids some day. So, what does she do but marry someone who is much older, divorced, has two children, and then she complains about her situation! Every time I hear her complain, I think to myself, "It's as if you've wanted to go to New York City your whole life, took the train to Chicago, and complain that you can't see plays on Broadway, go to a Yankees game or walk to Times Square!" I understand that "things happen," but we really do have more control over our own lives than we think we do and we just need to stay true to ourselves and make choices that support what we ultimately want in life. Relating this story to business, don't take a job as an accountant if you hate dealing with numbers, or take a job as a salesperson if you hate dealing with people!

I will share a personal story of how I became *lucky,* according to the new definition I described above—"when opportunity meets preparedness." Several years ago I worked as an account executive for a large telecommunications company selling business telephone systems. I was approaching the point where I needed to think about buying a new car because the lease on the car I was driving was about to expire. I thought about what kind of car I *really* wanted, and not just what I could afford. Well, I thought BMWs were pretty cool, so I cut out a picture of one and pinned it to my cubical wall as motivation. I soon realized that on my current salary and commission plan, I would, in fact, *not* be able to afford a BMW. So, plan B was to get another job that paid enough so I *could* afford a BMW! There was no reason I had to stay where I was, I was up for a new challenge, and I was simply curious to see if I could get the kind of job that would make it possible for me to drive a new BMW! So, I began doing research on the Internet for high-level sales job listings, compiled a *Career Results Portfolio,* and got to work hunting for a new job. To make a long story short, I accepted an offer as regional sales manager for a data cabling company at *twice* my base salary at the time and with a considerably better commission and annual bonus plan. Not only did I buy a new BMW within the first month at my new job, I also paid off years of credit card debt within six months, instead of the six years I had previously estimated it would take to pay it off had I stayed at my old job. The lesson here is, once you're clear on what you want, put your energy towards that, every day, and watch what happens as you lay the foundation for the future you truly desire.

ACTIVITY: Set Your Goal

Write down one goal you would like to achieve. Next to it, write a date that represents a deadline when you want to reach that goal. Then, determine what monthly, weekly, and daily activities will be necessary for you to do to meet your goal. (It is also a good idea to include an incentive or reward should you reach the goal in the time frame you've allotted. If the incentive or reward you've chosen is tangible, put a picture of it somewhere in plain view where you will see it every day.)

5

Selling Value vs. Price: It Isn't About the Money

Anytime you hear an objection to your proposal based on price, you haven't clearly defined the value of your solution. When true value is perceived by the prospect, price becomes a non-issue. However, when true value is *not* perceived by the prospect, price becomes a major issue. Therefore, it is necessary to understand your prospect's hot buttons and decision-making criteria before developing a solution and presenting your proposal.

The following tips will help you design solutions that will appeal to the majority of prospects' hot buttons including return-on-investment, profitability, and time and money savings.

- Sell profits, not products and services or features and benefits.
- Show the return-on-investment your solution will provide to your prospect including estimated dollars and timetable based on proven results you've provided for other clients.
- Determine the benefits of your solution and then tie dollars to it in terms of money or time saved by implementing your solution over time (i.e. show a monthly savings, quarterly savings, and annual savings your solution will provide to your prospect.)
- Design your proposal around *profit improvement* and include information that shows your proposal turns your solution into dollars for your customer.
- Show the sacrifice your prospect will make by *not* implementing your solution—paint a picture of the worst case scenario.

- Compare the one-time investment (and use the term *investment*, not *price* or *cost*) of your solution to the long-term savings your prospect will enjoy either in increased productivity, time savings, money savings, or all of the above.
- Come up with a payment plan to make your solution more affordable to your prospects. Break down payments into monthly or quarterly options and offer a discount for pre-payment.
- Become a problem-solver/solution provider for your prospects and clients.

When I sold telephone systems for a large telecommunications hardware vendor years ago, I was not allowed to let a proposal out the door without a section that specifically addressed the return-on-investment my solution would provide the prospect. I was able to show a time savings based on various features of the phone systems, which then equated to a dollar savings. We also had leasing programs available that made our phone systems more affordable. Oftentimes I was able to show that the monthly savings the new phone system would provide for the prospect exceeded the monthly lease payment. When you're able to show that the benefit or results of your solution outweigh the investment, you have accomplished selling value, not price, and you will win every time.

Below I have listed the common hot buttons of my prospects and addressed each one with the value and results The Blitz Experience™ solution provides.

Prospect Hot Button Value of Blitz Experience™ Solution

Sales training that changes behavior. Behavior Changing Blitz Campaign consists of three Blitzes forty-five days apart to allow sales reps to internalize the new techniques they've learned by practice and repetition to form new proactive selling habits.

Atmosphere that promotes learning. The Blitz Experience™ is fun yet requires actual prospecting activity from the sales reps the day of the training. Reps are provided incentives such as hourly prizes and snacks. Lunch is provided as well.

Return-on-investment is important. Results from working with other clients have shown an average return on investment of 2900 percent. (In other words, clients get up to twenty-nine times back in revenue what they invested in the program within ninety days of program facilitation.)

ACTIVITY: List the Hot Buttons of a Current Prospect and Address Each One with the Value and Results Your Solution Provides

6

Understanding the Difference Between an Application and an Opportunity and Suspects vs. Prospects

Often salespeople confuse an *application* for their products and services with an *opportunity* to sell their products and services. In other words, just because there is a fit, or application, for your products and services within any given organization, does not necessarily mean that there is opportunity to sell your products and services. Webster's dictionary defines an *application* as "the act of putting to a special use or purpose" while an *opportunity* is defined as "a favorable or promising combination of circumstances." Therefore, for our purposes here, the main difference between the two lies in the level of interest from the prospect, which you, in fact, have the ability to create.

Also, salespeople confuse *suspects* with *prospects*. Probably worth defining for clarification purposes, a *suspect* is someone you guess, or suspect, might be a good candidate for your products and services. A *prospect*, on the other hand, is someone who has already met a certain level of criteria or qualification and has shown interest in what you sell. With the above definitions of application, opportunity, suspect and prospect, you should begin to see a direct correlation, or obvious pairing, between applications and suspects, as well as opportunities and prospects. In other words, often *applications* of your products and services go hand in hand with the companies you *suspect* as candidates for your products and services. In contrast, once you've qualified a company to the *prospect* level, *opportunities* for your products and services begin to emerge.

Let's say, for example, that you sell CRM software (customer relationship management) that both helps companies to provide consistent, high-quality customer service to their customers and helps salespeople manage their prospect and customer database. While you may find a company with a large sales force who, based solely on the size of the sales force, seems a *suspect* for your software, until you can convert the *application* of your software into an *opportunity* to sell it, you are, as they say, dead in the water. The challenge then is to convert *suspects* into *prospects* and *applications* into *opportunities*.

Your test in this example is to convert the *application* of your CRM software into an *opportunity* to sell it to your prospect. By creating the interest of your prospect for your CRM software, you have created the opportunity to sell it.

Prospects don't know what they don't know and if you as a creative salesperson can tell your prospects what challenges they have that they're not aware of, you can then offer a solution to solve their challenge with your products and services. This, by the way, is a much more effective way of selling than looking only for prospects who know they have a need, for several reasons, which you will read more about in Part Two, Section Nine of this book, *Creating Opportunities Where They Don't Appear to Exist.*

ACTIVITY PART ONE: Describe an Application for Your Product or Service

ACTIVITY PART TWO: Describe an Opportunity for Your Product or Service

ACTIVITY PART THREE: Describe a Suspect for Your Product or Service

ACTIVITY PART FOUR: Describe a Prospect for Your Product or Service

Part Two: Generating Qualified Leads
Discovering Opportunities that Exist

7

21 Truths about Generating Qualified Leads (by Lee Marc Stein)

How many times have you received a lead and never followed up? Ever wonder why you didn't follow up? Oftentimes when I get a lead, I'm unsure of how qualified it is or if it's really a good fit as a prospect for my services, i.e. whether or not it fit my ICP. Until I came up with my Ideal Client Profile, I had no way of measuring whether or not a lead was a good lead. Now that you've created your ICP, use it as a guide each time you receive a lead. Do the research to answer the questions you need to have answered in order to determine whether or not it's a lead worth pursuing. Sometimes this may require calling the prospect directly, while other times doing research on the Internet by visiting the Web site of the lead may work, too.

In doing research for this book, I ran across some additional great tips for generating qualified leads from Lee Marc Stein, president of Lee Marc Stein Ltd., a direct marketing consulting and creative services firm. The twenty-one most significant truths he's learned in the last thirty-five years of being involved in the development and deployment of scores of business-to-business lead generation programs are as follows:

1. Separate suspects from prospects

Too many advertising/promotion dollars—and too much time—are spent on people who will never buy. Unless your lead generation advertising weeds these people out, it's not working effectively. It's putting a strain on those who process and follow up on leads. The media you select, the offers you make, your creative strategy, and even your tone all play key roles in drawing out high potential prospects and screening out suspects.

2. Sell the next step harder than you sell your product or service

The whole objective of lead generation programs is to begin the sales process, not to complete it. Your initial direct mail or e-mail should push for action on the next step—sending for more information, a free sample, a free analysis. Once you have qualified prospects, you can concentrate on a full presentation of product benefits, features, and applications.

3. Construct meaningful, actionable tests

No direct response program—whether executed in direct mail, e-mail, print, online or broadcast—can be improved without valid testing. Make sure you test the most significant factors first—lists/media and offers. Once you have a read of results, react quickly and incorporate them into your program. Your results analysis should not only include number of leads and cost per lead, but cost per appointment and per sale. Making decisions on lead costs alone can be disastrous.

4. Once is not enough

Give suspects more than a single time to qualify themselves. No matter how intrusive your direct mail package, e-mail, print ad or online ad, your target may miss it the first time around. Give prospects multiple opportunities to say yes to your offer, whether that means getting additional information, a price quote, or a call/visit from your sales representative. The more narrowly defined your market, the more time you have to spend on each prospect.

5. Support your mail

Direct mail is still a mainstay of business-to-business lead programs. If you decide to try mail, support it. If your mail package is an expensive, dimensional one, herald its arrival with a teaser package, e-mail blast, or print ad. If the mailing is relatively small, think about leaving a voicemail message with the recipient. For campaigns concentrated in particular cities, consider radio. After the mailing drops, follow it up with telemarketing, a quick mail reminder or an e-mail.

6. Support your sales force, distributors and wholesalers

Make sure they have full information on your campaigns—sample packages, copies of the print ads and e-mail messages, media utilized, launch dates. Keep them posted on results. An exciting "sell in" can be as important to your success as anything else you do.

7. Don't make it *too* easy to reply…

… if you want more *qualified* leads. Checking off a single box on a reply card and putting it in an outbound mail pickup may not a prospect make. Simply asking prospects to hit "reply" to your e-mail may not qualify them, either. Ask your prospects to fill in just a few lines of information and you'll boost the quality of your response without damaging quantity.

8. Let your prospects tell you how serious they are

Allow several options on your response form ranging from, "Have your representative call me immediately" to "No interest now. Call me in six months." Even the "no interest now" respondents are prospects.

9. ENVELOPE, please!

Unless your objective is to drive prospects to your Web site, it's unlikely that self-mailers or postcards are going to work for you. Yes, they're cheaper to produce, but the cost in lost opportunities is astronomical. In mailing to certain market segments, you need an envelope that indicates one-to-one correspondence—lasered, closed-face, with no teaser copy. Words like "Important," "Confidential," "New," or even "First Class Mail" can kill one-to-one perception. In most market segments, think of your envelope as a billboard for what's inside. Use sizes that will stand out in the mail. Test a strong offer or powerful benefit statement as teaser copy.

10. Plan separate creative strategies and offers for different levels of decision makers

Even if you're prospecting within a specific industry, copy and offer—and sometimes graphics—must change by function and by the objective of your communication. The highly technical approach you make to the head of the IT department will not work in addressing the CEO. And the CEO's possible interest in your product/service will differ from the CFO's.

11. Understand the "hot button"

Executives are much more often concerned about their time than about saving a few dollars. Direct mail/e-mail efforts that don't demand a lot of time and that demonstrate how the product/service can pay back hours work well to management segments. If the savings are enormous, that's a different story. And the best story is getting the recipient to believe responding is the first step in MAKING BIG MONEY. Middle managers may be more concerned about self-preservation (of their jobs) and about making a safe, unquestionable choice.

12. Test a survey approach, particularly with suspects

Carefully structured, a questionnaire mailing can help you learn more about your target audience and how to approach it with follow-up efforts. Surveys engage interest as they begin selling. If they're kept short, surveys can work in e-mail efforts as well.

13. Throw away the concept of response percentage

If your market universe is 1,000, a 2 percent response rate is totally insufficient. Standard direct mail will not suffice. You need to call as many media into play as possible. Your direct mail must be an "event in the mail box." That may involve creating and mailing hand-assembled cartons, sending out videos, or delivering a series of premiums by courier. On the other hand, in working with very large universes (or with a very small sales force), a 2 percent response may mean you haven't done a very good job of pre-qualifying prospects. You may be better off with a .5 percent response.

14. Use testimonials and case histories

Aside from the credibility they imbue, they provide the prospect with applications and usage guidance. Large corporations should select testimonials or case histories that emphasize the company's ability to provide fast, personal service. Smaller marketers should use endorsements reflecting on the company's strength and stability. Include testimonials that underscore how customers were rewarded by finding out more when they were prospects.

15. Peg your copy and offer on the life cycle stage of your product/service

If you're pioneering a new product, service or process, your efforts will have to do more education to get an appointment. If you're a new entry in an established category, you must convince prospects why they should even consider a switch.

16. When in doubt, play it straight

Humor and cuteness can cut through clutter in a business environment. However, if you have the slightest doubt about how the message will be received, play it safe and use a strong statement of benefits to break through.

17. Include a "keeper" in your mailings...

...particularly if you're planning only one mailing. We all want response immediately, but in most cases (98 percent) recipients have no need to respond at the moment. Give them something to remember you by after the "advertising" portion of your mailing has been discarded. It could be anything from a wallet-size calendar or tips for saving time or improving energy to a pad of post-it notes with your company's name on them.

18. Use premiums judiciously

The right premium increases response to your lead-generation efforts, and may even lower your cost per response. It also maintains conversions to appointments and sales. But overemphasizing the premium can bring you response from "freebie junkies." Select premiums with obvious value, but not enough value to be a bribe.

19. Test response lists.

Even though you're not selling directly through the mail, you ought to be testing response lists against the compiled lists you may be using. Proven willingness to open and respond to direct mail and e-mail solicitations is as important in lead generation as it is in direct selling. Controlled circulation publication lists help achieve the quantity of names you may be looking for.

20. Stretch your prospect base

If you're mailing to technical functions, or even to middle management types, test a routing slip (real or simulated) on the outer envelope. Also include a second response form in the package. It can add as much as 20 percent to results. If you're using e-mail, ask the recipient to forward it to appropriate parties within the company.

21. Transform gatekeepers into advocates

If you're mailing to upper management types, be aware that most of their mail is still screened by administrative assistants. To get your message on top of the pile (instead of in the circular file), address a message to the screeners explaining why the VIP should see your communication.

Lee Marc Stein, author of *21 Truths About Generating Qualified Leads,* can be reached at 631-724-3765 or lmstein@leemarcstein.com.

8

Finding Online Resources

I n addition to these wonderful tips from Lee Marc Stein, another invaluable resource I use is Hoover's, an online business information resource that gives all kinds of information either about a particular company or even a particular executive. It does the research for you and is a great tool to use when measuring a lead against your ICP. It even allows you to create prospect lists based on your ICP. Check it out at www.hoovers.com.

Additionally, Google news alerts and Biz Journals Search Watch are also fantastic resources. (Please see the ACTIVITIES below for information on how to sign up for a Google news alert and Biz Journals Search Watch specific to your needs.)

In my business, for example, it is important to know which companies have a *VP of Sales*, since they are typically the decision maker in regard to sales training, and a VP level indicates a certain sized company that would fit my ICP. Also, *Strategic Alliances* indicate the "dealer network" format that fits my ICP. I receive press release e-mails each day from Google that contain the words VP of sales (or vice president of sales) and Strategic Alliance. Since the press release usually has to do with the hiring or promotion of a VP of sales, or a new Strategic Alliance forming, that tells me the particular company is growing and has budget available in their sales department. It also gives me the name of my contact, the VP of Sales, or person in charge of the Strategic Alliance. Before calling the contact mentioned, I do my research in Hoover's and on the company Web site to understand more about their business such as the number of employees, number of sales reps, number of locations, and annual revenue. Once I determine the lead fits my ICP, I now have a reason to call the VP of sales or Strategic Alliance contact mentioned in the press release, congratulate him on the new position, and offer my sales training services to make him look good by way of helping him grow his business!

Other great online sales resources include www.sellingpower.com, www.salesandmarketing.com, www.lead411.com, www.bizjournals.com, and www.justsell.com.

Sometimes it's necessary to play detective and use a combination of the above mentioned resources to find the information you need. Let's say, for example, you have searched for a type of company in Google and found several Web sites that meet your search criteria. In researching the various companies you found through Google, you are unable to find the name of the appropriate contact. Once you have the name of the company for which you would like to have the appropriate contact name, you can then enter the company name in Hoover's to find the appropriate contact within the company.

ACTIVITY PART ONE: Create Your Own Google Alert

Go to www.google.com/alerts?t=1&hl=en. Create a Google Alert by reading the instructions and completing the information in the box to the right of the screen. Consider any "trigger events," for example, companies that are moving, have recently received funding, or that are hiring. Then type in the appropriate key words, relevant to your business, for the topic you wish to monitor. You can create as many Google alerts on as many different topics as you like. This is an excellent and *free* way to generate leads.

ACTIVITY PART TWO: Create Your Own Biz Journals Search

Go to http://www.bizjournals.com/account/register. Create a Biz Journals Search Watch by first registering and creating an account. This is a free service offered by Biz Journals which will track your customers, prospects, and competitors, and e-mail you when they appear in one of Biz Journals' articles. This service becomes a powerful tool that allows you to stay on top of the latest business news without having to do all the research yourself. You can create as many Search Watches as you like.

9

Creating Opportunities Where They Don't Appear to Exist

One of the most powerful things you can do as a sales professional is create opportunities where they don't appear to exist. This is true for a couple of reasons. First, by *creating* an opportunity, versus *responding* to it, you practically eliminate your competition. Think about it. If you create a need for your product or service within a prospect's organization that they didn't know they had, that means they are not actively looking for a vendor to provide the products and services you do. If you are the only one proposing a solution for the opportunity you have created, you have eliminated the number of choices for your prospect to make. In other words, either they purchase your solution or they don't, but at least the choice isn't between your solution and those of other multiple vendors. Also, chances are if you are the one who created the opportunity, or showed your prospect that they need your products or services, the prospect will look to you as a consultant rather than a salesperson, which creates a deeper level of trust. Even if the prospect decides to shop your solution, you can be involved in the process of naming the criteria for the solution, slanted of course to the strengths of your products and services, again making it difficult for the competition to compete. Your power to eliminate or reduce the competition is an important skill in winning more business and creating lasting relationships with your clients.

Secondly, when *creating* an opportunity, you become a *partner* with that prospect instead of a vendor, again, solidifying your relationship with the prospect. Shannon Kavanaugh of Go-To-Market Strategies[1] uses these four levels of sales to speak to the level of the prospect-salesperson relationship that I have included below.

- **Seller:** Onetime sale mentality
- **Vendor:** You're in the Rolodex for future possibility of business
- **Supplier:** Predictable repeat business
- **Partner:** Mutual dependence for business success

As a *seller* when relating to your prospects, the best you can hope for is a onetime sale, which means you'll need to start over every month in your sales efforts. However, moving up one level to a *vendor* relationship, you are considered as one of several other vendors (your competitors) for the possibility of future business. As a *supplier* you have the opportunity for predictable repeat business, and as a *partner* you create a mutual dependence for business success.

Obviously, the *partner* level is the best you can hope for and should be your goal with each and every prospect. Turning your prospects into *partners* creates lasting, predictable business with customers who depend on you for their business success. This type of customer relationship is the epitome of the *work smarter* mentality. Just think how much less effort it would take to have customers who think of you as a *partner* instead of a *seller*. It is much easier to sell more to an existing customer than it is to find a new customer, so why not make a conscious effort to create these *partner* relationships?

Okay, now that I've convinced you that the best methodology you can follow in terms of finding new business is to *create* opportunities, what you're probably wondering now is, *how* do I *create* opportunities?

The best way to describe *how* to do this is to provide a specific example of how I did this with my most recent *partner-client*, a regionally based insurance company.

[1] Shannon Kavanaugh is the president of Go-To-Market Strategies, www.gotomarketstrategies.com. Reach her at 206-547-2322 or shannonk@gtms-inc.com

This particular company was not *looking* for sales training. They were, however, open to talking with me to learn more about The Blitz Experience™ sales training program to determine whether or not there was a fit within their organization. I started, of course, by asking many open-ended questions so that I would have a good idea of how they were currently developing their business and finding new clients or selling more policies to existing clients. The interesting thing to me was that the insurance agents worked in an inbound call center responding to callers about insurance policies. This particular insurance company uses multiple mediums for advertising such as TV, direct mail, radio, and the like, and had done a good job creating brand recognition in the community, thus having a need for an inbound call center.

While their current inbound methodology was all well and good, my question to my contact was, *what would happen if you took your agents out of the inbound call center for a day and focused only on outbound calls?* This was a paradigm shift for this company because they had always been in the *response* mode in dealing with prospects, rather than a more proactive or outbound approach.

Because I created the opportunity with this particular prospect, who is now a *partner-client*, I had no competition. I had the opportunity to explain how The Blitz Experience™ sales training program would inspire and teach their agents to become more proactive in the approach, including outbound phone calls to develop prospects and new clients as a part of their sales approach.

The client was intrigued and decided to pilot the Blitz Experience™ program by having me facilitate it in three cities for sixty-five agents. At the conclusion of the pilot program, the agents had literally doubled the number of policies sold the day of the Blitz Experience™ training program. Obviously my client was thrilled with these results. Based on the outcome of the program, this client has changed the culture of their inbound call center and the methodology in which their agents go to market. Now, each agent takes himself out of the inbound queue once a week to focus only on outbound calls, using the techniques taught during The Blitz Experience™ program.

Since the pilot program, I have been retained to conduct seven more Blitz programs over the course of the next eight months. Based on the partner relationship I have with this client, not only is there more opportunity for additional Blitz programs, I will also have the opportunity to create new sales training programs for the client as well as speak and hold workshops at future sales conferences. This particular client has become a great case study for The Blitz Experience™ and has offered to be a reference for the program at any time with future prospects, all because the opportunity with this prospect was *created* and not just responded to.

ACTIVITY: Create an Opportunity That Doesn't Appear to Exist

Make a list of ten prospects with whom you are not currently working who fit your Ideal Client Profile as discussed earlier. Approach each of them with the *opportunity-creation methodology*. Ask open-ended questions (starting with *who, what, why, when, where, and how*) and/or make statements beginning with *please tell me about* or *please describe* to gather as much information as you can about the prospect in their own words. Make sure your questions are targeted around finding out what's lacking in the prospect's current situation for which you may be able to provide a solution. Based on the information gathered, develop your approach, create the opportunity, and present your solution to the suspect. Make a note of how many new *partner-clients* you are able to convert from the ten suspects with whom you started.

10

Networking

Networking for leads is a common way of finding new business. We go to an event, give our business cards to everyone we meet, and hope that the exchange will turn into some business. I have a couple of thoughts about networking that may seem a bit outside the norm, but consider this: when networking and asking for leads, first, GIVE a lead—what I like to call *Bestow Networking*. Begin the conversation by focusing on the other person. Ask questions about their business, what makes a good lead for them, and be specific. Consider questions you pose in your ICP and ask the same of those you might be able to help find leads. What industry are they targeting? What size companies are they looking to work with? What is the title of the person they usually deal with? As you're gathering this information, think of the people you know in your database of contacts that fit their ICP. You'll be amazed to see what will happen next after you've given a qualified lead or contact based on the answers to the specific questions you've asked. Chances are, you'll walk away with a few good leads too, as long as you're specific in telling the other person what makes a good lead for you, considering your ICP, of course.

While I have many stories I could share as examples of the effectiveness of this strategy, I'll share just three. The first happened several years ago when I was meeting with a local research company that was a prospect for my Blitz Experience™ sales training program. When I arrived and met my contact for the first time, the first words out of his mouth were, "I only have about ten minutes." After building rapport for a few minutes, I began asking questions about his business, mostly relating to their prospecting efforts to determine whether or not there was truly an opportunity for The

Blitz Experience™. The best question I asked was, "What makes a good lead for you?" After listening intently and taking a few notes, I realized I had several ideal contacts for him that I was able to share on the spot. By offering a couple of good leads for him, he immediately dropped his guard and suddenly found another hour and a half to spend with me, in spite of only having "ten minutes" to talk at the beginning of our meeting! Not only did he give me some great ideas for a new keynote program I was putting together, he also offered me several great leads!

Another great example of how well *Bestow Networking* works happened just recently. Kip, a colleague of mine, owns an online commercial real estate listing company that features comprehensive market coverage with listings of buildings, spaces, and subleases available from specific landlords and leasing agents. He sells subscriptions to service-oriented companies that sell to the commercial real estate industry. I personally introduced him to three business owner colleagues of mine and sang the praises of his service, encouraging them to consider signing up. Kip was thrilled to not only have three qualified leads, but personal introductions as well. Later, I wanted to get my foot in the door with a local broadband company and, as it turns out, the president of the company was Kip's cousin. I called Kip to ask for a personal introduction and he was more than happy to provide it!

Finally, keep in mind that networking doesn't always have to be about exchanging leads to sell the products and services you provide. It can also be a great way to find a job. Recently a colleague of mine was laid off from a sales position with an information and printing solutions company. She invited me to lunch to talk about the next steps in her career and was hoping I could help her with making contact with potential employers. As it turned out, I did know several companies looking to hire new salespeople at the time, so I made several introductions to position her with the right people in each of the companies. I also offered to e-mail her resume to my contacts database in an effort to get the word out that she was looking for a new job. In doing this for her, I expected nothing in return. She is a colleague and friend, as well as a hard worker, and I felt that any organization would be lucky to have her. The interesting thing is that while none of the job leads or connections I provided her panned out, she did find a new job as a project manager. Coincidently, her new employer was one of the companies I was targeting as an ideal client for my sales training program, The Blitz Experience™. A few weeks into her job, she sent me an e-mail asking how she might be able to help me make contact with the appropriate decision maker at her company regarding sales training. She has since given me several contacts to help get the sales process started and continues to update me on the internal goings-on in case any of the internal activity might drive the need for sales training.

The bottom line is that when we help other people and don't expect anything in return, often we do get something in return. It may not be right away, it may not be ever, but many times at some point that person we helped will remember and want to help us when we have a need at some point in the future.

ACTIVITY: Give Five Leads

List the top five colleagues, outside of your own organization, who you network with on a regular basis. Next to each, write several of the criteria that make up their ICP. Next, review your database for leads that fit your colleague's ICP. Then, write down the contact information of a lead you have for each of them within your current database that matches their ICP. Give each of your top five contacts the lead you have written down. Watch what happens in the next two to three weeks after giving these leads!

ICP Based Networking

ICP based networking refers to asking people you network with for contacts at companies you've already identified as fitting your ICP. So, for example, if I wanted to get into Coca-Cola, I'd ask people, "What contacts do you have in the sales department at Coca-Cola?" Even if the people I ask don't have any *sales contacts* at Coca-Cola, they might know *someone* at Coca-Cola or even *someone who knows someone* who works at Coca-Cola. When networking, just getting your foot in the door at a particular company you want to work with is enough to get the ball rolling. Let's say I am referred to someone in the accounting department at Coca-Cola. Although I don't work with the accounting department when selling my sales training programs, the person in accounting at Coca-Cola may have a sales contact for me there. Once I get the name of the appropriate person in sales at Coca-Cola, I can now use the name of the referring person in accounting as a reference. By being specific when networking, you make it easy for others to help you. You have to help people help you in order to get the kind of leads that best fit your ICP. Remember, the more specific you are when asking for leads, the better outcome you'll have with the leads you receive.

ACTIVITY: Get Five Leads

Based on your ICP, make a list of five prospects/companies you would like to be, but are not currently, doing business with. Based on the previous ACTIVITY, after you've *given* leads to your top five colleagues and you've waited the two or three weeks as suggested, call each of your colleagues and ask if they have any contacts or know anyone who has contacts at each of the five ideal prospects you've listed. If they are unable to help you with this, ask for one lead from each of them, based on your ICP. If you've given leads based on your colleague's ICP, it is likely your colleagues will make an effort to help you as well.

Ideal Referral Partner Profile (IRPP)

The Ideal Referral Partner Profile (IRPP) refers to the criteria that make up your Ideal Referral Partner. Referral partners take networking to a new level. A referral partner is someone who is committed to partnering with you to share leads, referrals, and personal introductions. It often implies an exclusive relationship. In other words, let's say you have a referral partner who works for a commercial moving company. I suggest you only network with ONE referral partner from a commercial moving company. This promotes loyalty in that the commercial moving company contact you work with works exclusively with you, and no one else from your industry. Take the time to share your ICP with your referral partner and be sure you understand their ICP as well. The ICP becomes a valuable tool when measuring leads and opportunities you come across for each other.

ACTIVITY: Choose Your Ideal Referral Partner

Choose your Ideal Referral Partner by answering the questions below.

What colleague in my network, that I currently exchange leads with on a regular basis, has virtually the same ICP as I do?

What industry does he represent?

What is the product or service that my colleague offers and how or why does it complement what I sell?

Is there, or could there be, a perceived "value-add" in offering my colleague's products and services to my clients, and offering my products and services to my colleague's clients?

Mutual Endorsement Mailer

Once you have identified your Ideal Referral Partner, consider doing a mutual endorsement mailer. A mutual endorsement mailer is a marketing tool used not only to promote each other's businesses, but to actually make personal introductions for each other. Here's how it works. Review your contact database with your referral partner and determine which of your contacts best fits your referral partner's ICP. Next, on *your* letterhead, have your referral partner write a letter to the contacts in your database to personally introduce your referral partner to your contacts who have been identified as fitting your referral partner's ICP. Your referral partner is writing a letter on your letterhead, as if it is coming from you, as a way of being personally introduced to specific contacts in your database. By having your referral partner write the letter, he will be able to stress the key points he wants to convey to those receiving the letter.

Also include any marketing material that is relevant to your referral partner's business, as well as your business card and your referral partner's business card. Remember, you should sign the letter, as it is coming from you. Have your referral partner do the same for you, on his letterhead, with his signature, introducing you to the contacts in his database that fit your ICP. About a week after the mailers have been sent, call the contacts who have received the mutual endorsement mailer given to you by your referral partner. When you call, say, "I'm calling to follow up on the letter you received from David Smith." (David Smith being your referral partner.) From there, the conversation should flow fairly smoothly and you now have a great introduction into a new prospective opportunity! Below is an example of a mutual endorsement letter I have written for my referral partner, Bob Jones, to send to those contacts in his database that meet my ICP.

"Since our Sittig Northwest Blitz Program, we have gone from 23% of plan to 105% of plan! Our sales reps have changed their behavior to include consistent, proactive selling activities that have resulted in tremendous revenue growth for our company." VP Sales, Telecommunications Company

John Doe
ABC Company
123 Main Street
City, State, Zip

Dear John,

I am writing today to personally introduce you to Andrea Sittig-Rolf, Puget Sound Business Journal columnist and CEO of Sittig Northwest, Inc. Sittig Northwest is the developer and exclusive provider of an activity-based prospecting skills training program called The Blitz Experience™.

Featured on SellingPower.com in May, 2004, the Prospecting Blitz Experience™ Program is designed to promote lead generation and pipeline development for companies such as yours interested in creating and maintaining consistent sales results. This program is perfect as part of a 'best-practice' process, when entering a new market, as part of a new-hire sales program, or to simply build the sales pipeline with new opportunities. The Blitz Experience™ will not only motivate your sales team to learn and practice proactive selling habits, but will also generate substantial revenue for your bottom line! The Sittig Northwest Blitz Experience™ Program is designed to motivate your sales team to make outbound telephone calls to schedule appointments and generate qualified leads resulting in additional clients and additional revenue.

Because the program includes a Pre-Blitz assignment, sales reps are prepared for a successful Blitz, allowing them to focus on the activities that drive tremendous results in just one day.

Here is what one of her clients has said about The Blitz Experience™ Program:

> *"I really liked being a part of The Blitz Experience™. I and others could really see the energy in the air. In just one day, we had great success: 651 calls, 120 quotes and 40 sales, that's double our typical daily production…WOW!!!!!!"* Manager, Insurance Company

Please accept a call from Andrea Sittig-Rolf next week to answer any questions you may have and to schedule a brief meeting. In the meantime, please feel free to visit www.sittignw.com for more information. Thank you!

Sincerely,

Bob Jones
XYZ Company, *(Referral Partner to Andrea Sittig-Rolf)*.

Sittig Northwest, Inc. is a results oriented, interactive sales program and new business development firm that helps companies increase sales through the creation and implementation of effective Blitz Experience™, Team Building and Lead Generation Programs.

You may have noticed that I included a couple of quotes from clients both at the top of the letter and near the end of the letter. When other clients have something positive to say about you and your company, it is the most powerful sales tool you have so use it. Be sure the quote you use speaks to the *results* you've created for your client, as this will give you credibility and inspire confidence in the prospect that you will deliver the same for him. Also, be sure to include any other titles or accolades that will give your company credibility. For example, not only am I the CEO of Sittig Northwest, Inc., but also a columnist with The Puget Sound Business Journal. Also, The Blitz Experience™ was featured on SellingPower.com's Web site homepage so I included that tidbit as well. If you can establish credibility early on in your letter, it is more likely the prospect will read it the entire way through.

Finally, keep your letter to one page. You want to create enough curiosity about who you are and what you do that the prospect will accept your follow-up phone call, but you don't want to tell everything there is to tell in the mutual endorsement introductory letter.

The mutual endorsement mailer is a very effective way to generate new business and takes simply giving or getting a referral to the next level!

ACTIVITY: Write Letter for Your Mutual Endorsement Mailer

Create the letter you would like your referral partner to send to introduce you to his clients that fit your ICP. Consider the template below when writing your letter, or refer to the example above for the letter I use for my Mutual Endorsement Mailer. (Remember that although you are writing the letter, it should be printed on your Referral Partner's company letterhead and signed by your Referral Partner as if it was written by your Referral Partner.)

"Testimonial from a satisfied client including specific results you have provided." Title, Company Name of person who stated the above testimonial.

John Doe
ABC Company
123 Main Street
City, State, Zip

Dear John,

I am writing today to personally introduce you to **_Your Name_** , **_Your Title_** of **_Your Company Name_**, *20–25 word unique description of your company and its mission in providing products or services to its clients.*

Explain the potential applications and benefits of your products and/or services.

State the reason(s) why this prospect should consider taking your call and scheduling a meeting with you when you follow up after sending this letter. Next, write "Here is what one of **Your Company Name** clients has said about their products and/or services:"

> **"***Testimonial from a satisfied client including specific results you have provided.***"** *Title, Company Name of person who stated the above testimonial.*

Please accept a call from **Your Name** next week to answer any questions you may have and to schedule a brief meeting. In the meantime, please feel free to visit **Your Web site** URL for more information. Thank you!

Sincerely,

Your Referral Partner's Name
Your Referral Partner's Company Name

Leveraging Referral Partners

Wouldn't it be great to not only get a referral, but to then leverage the source of that referral throughout the entire sales process to help you close the sale? Often we accept a referral from someone and work the opportunity ourselves, without realizing the power of the relationship our referral source has with the person they referred us to. By simply keeping the referral source informed of your progress with the referral you were given, you subtly empower that referral source to help you close the deal. Here's how it works.

Let's say Bob is the source of my referral and he refers me to Mike at ABC Company. I call Mike, schedule an appointment, and meet with him to determine his sales training needs. After meeting with Mike, I contact Bob to thank him, again, for the referral and let him know how my meeting went with Mike. Next, I present the proposal to Mike and he wants to "think about it." Okay, now I'm stuck, right? It's the old "I want to think about it" put off. So, I contact Bob and bring him up to speed regarding my progress with Mike and then, here's the kicker: I simply ask Bob's opinion as to what I should do next to move Mike from "I'll think about it" to "Let's make a deal!" Chances are, Bob will offer to see what he can do to help move Mike towards making a buying decision for my sales training offering. Now, instead of me doing the selling, Bob is doing it for me!

Now, I want to clarify a few different levels of referrals so that we are on the same page and can examine the best type of referral relationships to pursue. Ultimately, we want to work towards leveraging a specific type of referral relationship to gain the most effective strategy when developing new business. You may think that what I am about to explain is obvious, but it is necessary to get to the point so stay with me.

First, a basic referral is sometimes confused with what is better known as a lead. The difference is that while a basic referral indicates a close professional relationship and the ability to use the name of the person who referred you when contacting a new prospect, a lead is simply information that your referral source has shared with you.

For example, if I shared information with you about an opportunity to sell your products and services to a client of mine and told you to use my name as a reference when making contact, that is a *basic referral*. However, if I simply shared the information with you that there was an opportunity to sell your products and services to a client of mine, but did not allow you to use my name as a reference, that is a *lead*. Obviously, in this case, a basic referral is better than a lead.

Another type of referral is what's known as a *personal introduction*. The difference is that while a *basic referral* allows you to use the name of the person who referred you when contacting the prospect, a *personal introduction* means your referral source is going to make contact with the prospect for you, on your behalf, which is even better than a *basic referral*. So, to recap, we have three levels of referrals: a *lead,* a *basic referral,* and a *personal introduction*.
It should now be apparent that the type of referral you want to focus on is the *personal introduction*. Not only is it the most effective strategy when developing new business, it more closely ties your referral source to the entire sales process with that particular prospect. Let me explain.

Recently I was personally introduced to a prospect in the telecommunications industry. My referral source spoke with the prospect before introducing me to tell her about my Blitz Experience™ sales training program. The prospect was interested in hearing more so my referral source scheduled a time for the three of us to meet for lunch. Not only did my referral source introduce me to the prospect, she then proceeded to rave about the results my program had created for other Blitz Experience™ clients.

After the initial meeting, the prospect wanted more information about the specifics of The Blitz Experience™ so we met at her office where I could present the details of the program. She then requested a proposal based on her specific needs which I presented a few days later. A day or so after sending the proposal, I followed up by sending an e-mail to the prospect and did not get a response. Then, a few days later, I called her and left a voicemail message, and still did not receive a response.

Okay, now here's where it gets really interesting. Next, I contacted my referral source to bring her up to speed as to the status of where I was with the prospect she had introduced me to. Without having to ask for her help, she offered to find out more and get back to me. As it turns out, the prospect was, in fact, planning to retain my services for training, but needed to run it by one more person in the office before signing the contract and issuing a check request for the deposit. She hadn't responded to me yet because she didn't have a definitive answer on whether or not she was ready to move forward. The call from my referral source to the prospect acted as a reminder that the prospect needed to get back to me.

Without my having to call the prospect again, she called to tell me the good news—that she was ready to sign on the dotted line and issue a check for the deposit.

The point is that by keeping my referral source in the loop during the sales process, especially when I felt stuck, not only was she appreciative to know I had followed through with the referral she gave me, she was generous enough to offer to help me close the deal.

Many times, just by sharing with your referral source the status of the progress you've made with a particular prospect to whom you've been introduced, you will inspire your referral source to help you throughout the entire sales process.

So now your question probably is, okay great, personal introduction referrals are the best, but how do I get more of them? Here's what I suggest. The next time you get a lead or basic referral from a referral source, simply thank them and then ask the question, "Would you mind *introducing* me to the prospect?" Simple, I know, but just try it and see what happens.

ACTIVITY: Leverage Your Referral Partner or Referral Source

Choose a recent referral you've received from either a referral partner or referral source. Begin keeping your referral partner or source informed as to your progress with the prospect they've referred you to and especially let them know if you get "stuck" in the process to determine how they can best help you move the prospect forward in the sales process to the close.

Networking Events

Have you ever gone to a networking event that had a guest speaker and noticed the line of people waiting to talk to the speaker *after* the event? Were you one of the people standing in that line, blending in with the crowd of people hoping for the same thing? Oftentimes the reason people are motivated to meet the speaker *after* the event is that they hope to gain further insight regarding the topic that was presented, or they realize the speaker is a good person to know, either in terms of their own networking or prospecting efforts. Let me explain how effective it can be to meet the speaker *before* the event by offering a couple of examples from my own experience.

Several months ago I attended a Washington Software Alliance marketing meeting. I made a point to meet the speaker before the event to introduce myself and tell him a little more about my sales training company. His topic was specific to sales and marketing techniques for the high-tech industry. At the end of his keynote, he pointed me out to the entire room of people and said, "And to those of you who need sales training, this is Andrea, the sales trainer in the group!" How great was that? Free advertising for my company as well as a personal introduction by the keynote speaker to everyone in the room!

Recently I attended a networking event called *Marketing Strategies for Early Stage Companies* sponsored by MIT (Massachusetts Institute of Technology). From a networking perspective, the companies represented in the audience were prospects for my sales and marketing consulting offering. Often early stage companies need additional, part-time sales and marketing expertise to help them begin marketing their company's products and services to the marketplace. Because the speaker represented a software manufacturing company with a large international dealer network of salespeople and was a marketing executive within the organization, making his company and him a prospect for The Blitz Experience™, it made sense for me to meet him ahead of time. I made a point to introduce myself about fifteen minutes before the event was to begin. He asked me questions about my company and was intrigued by the concept of The Blitz Experience™. So intrigued, in fact, that during his presentation, he used my company and me as an example six times in just forty-five minutes! Basically this was free advertising since he was speaking to a room full of my potential prospects! Sure enough, the line of people waiting to speak to me after the event was as long as the line of people waiting to speak to him! People in the audience were more motivated to approach me because they were curious as to why the speaker used me as an example so much throughout the program. This was a great opportunity for me to talk to the people who approached me and further qualify them as prospects.

Taking this concept a step further, you can send a letter to the speaker before the event to introduce yourself, as well as your products and services, and let the speaker know you will be coming to the event where he is presenting. I tried this recently and had great results. I was planning to attend a seminar about cold calling, which was great since the audience members were there to learn about cold calling techniques and I teach a sales program about that very topic. I sent a letter in a 9X12 red envelope to the speaker and wrote on the back flap, "I'm looking forward to your seminar next week!" The seminar had an audience of 200+ people. Again, the speaker used me as an example in front of the audience by holding up the envelope I had sent, saying what a great idea this was as a "foot in the door" with the speaker. He then continued to use me as an example and asked me to help him on stage with a handshake exercise. As a result of this, I was able to give a thirty second commercial to the group about my company, and again, had many approach me after the seminar who wanted more information about my products and services.

When using this technique, I recommend sending a letter in the mail versus e-mail, since we are all bombarded with e-mail these days. Using a large, brightly colored envelope also works well, as long as it corresponds with your company branding message and you're able to use a company logo mailing label on the front of the envelope. On the back flap of the envelope, write something such as, "I'm looking forward to seeing your presentation at the ABC event 12.3.05." In other words, you want to *handwrite* your note and reference the name and date of the event. This will likely spark curiosity and motivate the recipient to open and read the letter you've sent. Taking this extra step may make it easier for you to approach the speaker at the event before the presentation, and it's likely you'll be remembered!

ACTIVITY (Option 1): Write Letter to Keynote Speaker

Check your calendar for the next networking event you plan to attend that features a keynote speaker. Write a letter introducing yourself and your company and let the speaker know the following: that you plan to attend the event where she is speaking, you're looking forward to the event and you will introduce yourself at the event. Send it in a 9X12 envelope and write on the upper back flap, at the top of the envelope, "I'm looking forward to meeting you at *ABC event!*" Once at the event, introduce yourself to the speaker *before* she delivers the keynote, if at all possible, and sit up front. If it's not possible to meet the speaker before the event, be the first in line *after* the event!

ACTIVITY (Option 2): Introduce Yourself to Keynote Speaker Before the Event

Skip sending the letter before the event and simply introduce yourself to the speaker at the event, before she delivers the keynote.

11

Appreciating the Power of Cold Calling

I know, I know, as high-level, professional salespeople, we hate cold calling! While I understand the general loathing of cold calling, think of it as a necessary evil, if you must. Don't discount the effectiveness of cold calling. All deals have to start somewhere, and while cold calling isn't necessarily the best way to start the sales or engagement process with a prospect, it is one way, and done consistently, can make up a significant percentage of your business! For example, at any given time when I analyze my pipeline, I typically find my prospects come from referrals 50 percent of the time and cold calling 50 percent of the time. Given that, my business would literally be half what it is today without cold calling.

The other reason I highly recommend cold calling as a supplement to your other new business development activities, is that it keeps you sharp. No other forum besides cold calling offers the opportunity, yes, *opportunity*, to practice overcoming common objections using your sense of humor and thinking fast on your feet, and it's a great learning experience. Over time, if done consistently, you will get better at it. The call reluctance you may have will go away eventually if you do it often enough and begin to have some positive results.

Getting Past the Gatekeeper

Receptionist: "ABC Company, how can I direct your call?"
Salesperson: "Hi, my name is Andrea Sittig-Rolf and I'm with Sittig Northwest. I'd like to talk to your sales manager please."
Receptionist: "Can I tell him what this is regarding?"
Salesperson: "Sure. We are the developer and exclusive provider of a sales training program called The Blitz Experience™ and I'd like to set up a time to meet with him to determine whether or not this program will be of benefit to ABC Company."
Receptionist: "Is he expecting your call?"
Salesperson: "Well, no, not exactly."
Receptionist: "Hold please."
Sales Manager's Voicemail: "Hi. I can't take your call right now so please leave a message and I'll call you back as soon as possible."

Sound familiar? Ever get the feeling the receptionist has been trained just to screen your calls and keep you away from connecting with your prospect at her company? Well, guess what, she has!

Conversations like the above haunted me in the early years of my sales career. After dealing with this same conversation over and over again, I decided there must be a better way so I started to experiment. Here's what I learned: The receptionist can either make or break you in any organization. She holds the key to your success in terms of actually directing you to the person you want to talk to in her organization. I've said "her company" and "her organization" previously because as far as you are concerned, it is *her* company. (Or his company if you're dealing with a male receptionist.) The point is, that knowing this, there are a few things you can do.

First, engage the receptionist. Then, be genuine in your approach. Receptionists can smell a rat from hundreds of miles away—that's part of their training, too.

Many times, just by logging on to a company Web site, you can find the name of the CEO or president of the company. Make note of this before making your call. Let's say the CEO of the company you're calling on is

John Jones. Now, let's take a look at how the conversation with the receptionist should go:

Receptionist: "ABC Company, how can I direct your call?"
Salesperson: "Hi, my name is Andrea Sittig-Rolf and I'm with Sittig Northwest. I'm hoping you can help me. I'm looking for the person in your organization who would make a decision regarding sales training. That wouldn't be John Jones, would it?"
Receptionist: "Oh no, that wouldn't be John Jones, that would be Bob Smith."
Salesperson: "Great! Can I speak to Bob, please?"
Receptionist: "Sure, I'll transfer you."
Salesperson: "Thank you."

Believe it or not, most of the time this technique works and will get you to the person you need to talk to. The idea is that the receptionist doesn't want to bother John Jones, the CEO, with a cold call from a salesperson. It's almost a relief for her to be able to transfer you to Bob Smith, someone below John Jones on the org chart at the company. Even if you are unable to speak to Bob Smith during this particular phone call, at least now you have the name of the person you need to talk to for the next time you call. Receptionists don't screen calls as much when you have the name of the person you want to talk to.

On another note, I know it seems obvious, but for goodness sake, say please and thank you! You would not believe the salespeople I've trained who don't even say "please" and "thank you" when dealing with receptionists, or anyone else for that matter. Simple courtesy goes a long way.

In the situation where you are talking to someone other than the receptionist who you realize is not the decision maker, and they tell you, "I'm not the one to talk to regarding your products or services." Do not say, "Oh, well who is?" Instead say, "Really? What is it you do?" and again, engage the person in conversation for a bit before asking who you should talk to instead.

Another tip is to ask for the sales department when the receptionist answers. Believe me, callers are not screened when calling on the sales department, for obvious reasons. Then, when you get a salesperson on the phone, say something like, "Hi. I'm not sure if you can help me, but I'm actually hoping to talk to your sales manager. Who would that be?" Salespeople are not trained to screen calls and we love to talk, so chances are you'll get plenty of information about the company you're calling on as well as the person you ultimately need to talk to.

Finally, when the receptionist answers, you can also try asking for the accounting department or accounts receivable department. You won't get screened by the receptionist from those departments and people in those departments aren't trained to screen calls, so chances are, they'll give you the information you need! But whatever you do, don't ask to be transferred to accounts payable.

ACTIVITY: Practice Getting Past the Gatekeeper

Create a list of suspects (those companies you suspect might become a prospect for your products and services once qualified). Choose companies you do NOT have a contact name for so you can practice getting past the gatekeeper using the techniques described above.

Tracking Call Ratios

An excellent way to measure your results from cold calling is to keep a record of your calls and track your success. For example, I have created a form called *The Blitz Numbers Tracking Worksheet* (please see Appendix E) that tracks calls, connects, appointments, proposals, and sales. Take a look at the *Blitz Numbers Tracking Worksheet* (Appendix E) and I'll explain each section.

Calls

Calls are defined as each time you dial the phone, whether you reach anyone or not; if you've dialed, you count it as a "call" on your form. (If your focus is that of outside sales, the purpose of tracking your outbound calls is to determine your *pro-active, outbound activities* as they relate to sales. If the main focus of your job requires that you handle *incoming* calls, you can also use this form to track the inbound calls you receive.)

Connects

Connects are defined as actually talking to the decision maker. Leaving a voicemail does not count, unless the decision maker calls you back and you actually have a conversation, in which case it then counts as a connect. Also, leaving messages with receptionists or assistants doesn't count as a connect either.

Appointments

This section is pretty self-explanatory: when you schedule an appointment you complete a bubble in the appointments section.

Call Backs

Call backs are defined as calls that come in as a result of leaving a voicemail message for the prospect. Tracking this will help you determine how effective you are at leaving voicemail messages that get a response from prospects, and is an important element in your call tracking ratios.

No

You should also consider tracking the number of times you hear no when making your calls. Why on earth would you want to track every time you hear the word "no" from a prospect? Well, believe it or not, counting the nos is equally important to counting your sales! How else will you know how often you typically hear no before you hear yes? Hearing no is a very real part of the selling process, so it's important to know your personal "no ratio" so that you can realistically plan your cold calling activities each week.

Proposals

In this section you complete a bubble when you've had the opportunity to propose your solution or quote a price on your product or service.

Sales

And of course, when you make a sale, you complete a bubble in this section.

After tracking your calls for ninety days, add up the columns from each worksheet to understand your daily ratios, then add those up to understand your weekly call ratios, monthly ratios, ninety-day ratios, and so on. In ninety days time, you should have a pretty good idea of your personal ratios. While this data will show you what your numbers are, based on your current skill level, (and simply by increasing the number of outbound calls you make, you can improve your sales ratio), you can also improve your *skill level* when making your calls. A great resource to increase your effectiveness when making cold calls is a book by Stephan Schiffman called *Cold Calling Techniques (That Really Work!)* 5th Edition. In his book, Mr. Schiffman clearly describes an easy to follow, step-by-step methodology for making *effective* cold calls and offers some invaluable techniques to help improve your sales ratios, based on improving your actual sales skills versus simply making more calls. The book is available on Amazon.com and should be available at your local bookstore. It is the best I've found for the subject of cold calling.

ACTIVITY: Track Your Call Ratios

Make photocopies of *The Blitz Numbers Tracking Worksheet* in Appendix E and track your own call ratios for ninety days to understand your personal call ratios. Use the *getting past the gatekeeper* techniques described in the previous section as you make your calls. For more information on how to improve your call ratios, buy Stephan Schiffman's book, *Cold Calling Techniques (That Really Work!)* 5th Edition. If you *sell* your product or service over the phone, rather than schedule appointments face-to-face, remove the "appointments" section of the worksheet and buy Stephan Schiffman's book, *Telesales*, for more information on how to improve your selling-over-the-phone ratios.

12

Conducting a Prospecting Blitz

Conducting a prospecting Blitz with your sales team is an excellent way to generate leads, create enthusiasm, and promote friendly competition among the salespeople. The beauty of a Blitz lies in the energy it creates and the "we're all in this together" attitude it inspires among teammates. The Blitz also stimulates practicing new and different prospecting techniques and requires that salespeople actually do the prospecting activity *during the course of the Blitz*. The salespeople not only learn new techniques, but they practice them on real prospects.

This methodology for prospecting is so effective that I've created a business out of it. In the past three years, I have become known as *The Blitz Master*, leading and encouraging thousands of salespeople to prospecting success. Here I will share this powerful prospecting methodology with you and I encourage you to either conduct your own prospecting Blitz or contact Sittig Northwest, Inc. to create and implement a Blitz just for your team at www.sittignw.com.

The Sittig Northwest, Inc. Blitz Experience™ Programs are interactive training programs designed to bring both structure and fun to prospecting and lead generation when working with sales teams.

Programs include:
- **Cold Call Blitz** – Empowers and motivates your team to make outbound cold calls.
- **Referral Blitz** – Promotes referral marketing and relationship leveraging techniques.

- **Cross Selling Blitz** – Encourages salespeople to sell more products and services to the same customer(s).

- **Strategic Alliance Blitz** – Blitz conducted for you and one strategic partner. Designed to double the sales opportunities for you and your strategic partner.

- **Vendor Sponsored Blitz** – Your vendors pay for the opportunity to participate in your Blitz, sponsoring hourly prizes and sharing the cost of your Blitz with other participating vendors, making it free for the client.

What results can you expect?

The Prospecting Blitz Program has helped many companies with their sales efforts and here's what some of them are saying:

"This program was a great investment of our marketing dollars and has exceeded my expectations! You really brought the team together. Three salespeople generated thirty-six leads plus three bookings in just four hours of outbound calls!"

CEO, Cruises and Events Company

"In reviewing the cold call Prospecting Blitz results after the day of our Blitz, I realize that without it we would not have accomplished the same results on our own. Ninety-one appointments and seventeen new accounts after conducting at three phase Prospecting Blitz is simply amazing! Our salespeople have actually changed their behavior to include consistent prospecting activity resulting in tremendous revenue for our company."

Sales VP, Telecommunications Company

"The team learned something about the statistics behind cold calling (i.e. how many calls they need to make to reach how many people to set appointments). They also learned some valuable techniques on how to leave effective voicemail messages that get returned."

Manager, Network Services Provider

ACTIVITY: Conduct Your Own Prospecting Blitz
The step-by-step process for conducting your own Blitz Program:

STEP 1: Plan your Blitz
- Determine the best application for your version of The Prospecting Blitz Program. Consider the following options:
  - **New Product/Service Launches.** Use The Prospecting Blitz Program to provide structure around your product introductions to prospects and existing customers.
  - **Event Promotion.** Do you have a seminar coming up? Or, are you attending any tradeshows you'd like to secure appointments for?
  - **New Hire Program.** Conduct a Blitz for your team of newly hired salespeople once they have learned about the products and services you offer.
  - **Pipeline Development and Ongoing Sales Results.** Having regularly scheduled prospecting Blitzes (one or two per month) is a great way to continue to fill your sales pipeline.
  - **Sales Channel Development.** Sponsor a Blitz Program for your Value Added Resellers and Channel Partners to create customer loyalty and encourage the sale of your products and services.
- Decide on your Blitz facilitator (should you wish to hire an outside facilitator, visit www.sittignw.com). Have your Blitz facilitator study this blueprint in detail, as well as the book *Cold Calling Techniques (That Really Work!)*, to get familiar with the material. Keep in mind your facilitator needs to be very enthusiastic and have a motivating personality.
- Determine your Blitz participants and schedule a full day for the Blitz.

STEP 2: Purchase necessary Blitz materials
- Blitz Agenda (See Appendix D)
- Prize Flyer (See Appendix D)
- Blitz Numbers Tracking Worksheet (See Appendix E)
- Book: *Cold Calling Techniques (That Really Work!)* 5th Edition by Stephan Schiffman (Order one for each Blitz participant. Available at www.amazon.com)
- Cold Calling Books Quiz (See Appendix F)

- Prizes: One Grand Prize of $100 value and four Hourly Drawing Prizes of $15 value each
- Getting the Appointment Poster (Available at www.sellingpower.com)
- The Crying Towel (available at www.sittignw.com)
- Index Cards (used in hourly prize drawing)
- Call Lists (Either from your own database or a newly purchased list) (Try www.lead411.com or www.infousa.com as potential sources for lists, or your own lists from tradeshows, current customer database or prospects database.)
- Candy, Prize Drawing Bowl, and Horns
- Optional items: Bottled water, morning snacks, and lunch in-house

NOTE: Don't have time to acquire the Blitz materials? Sittig Northwest's *The Prospecting Blitz Kit* contains everything you need to facilitate a Blitz for ten salespeople and is available at www.sittignw.com

STEP 3: Send out Pre-Blitz assignment letter to Blitz participants

One week before the Blitz, send your Blitz participants a copy of the book *Cold Calling Techniques (That Really Work!)* along with the following introductory letter:

> Dear Sales Superstar:
>
> We will be having a Prospecting Blitz [Enter date and time of Blitz] at [Enter place of Blitz].
>
> In order to prepare for the Blitz, please read this book in its entirety and know the material well enough to be quizzed during our pre-Blitz meeting beginning at [Enter start time of pre-Blitz meeting] in [Enter place of pre-Blitz meeting].
>
> This easy-to-read book is the best at providing the concept of how to make successful prospecting calls and covers the specific techniques involved in understanding the metrics, developing the script, and handling common objections.
>
> Using Chapter 4: Cold Call Mechanics, pages 135–140, create the call script you will use during our Blitz. Please be sure to bring your script with you to our pre-Blitz meeting.

Pay close attention to Chapter 2: By the Numbers. It is important you understand *your personal* conversion numbers, such as "how many calls" will lead to "how many appointments" will lead to "how many proposals" will lead to "how many closed sales" will lead to "how many dollars!"

You will have a form on the day of the Blitz that will help track your numbers, allowing you to ultimately understand how many calls you need to make to reach your account and income goals. Remember that as a salesperson, unlike any other career, YOU are in control of your income. Knowing your personal numbers is a key factor in determining your income.

Thanks for your commitment to this. It will be fun!

Happy reading!

[Enter your facilitator's name]
Blitz Facilitator (or *Blitz Master*)

STEP 4: Conduct your pre-Blitz meeting with all participants

On the morning of the Blitz, conduct a pre-Blitz meeting to introduce The Prospecting Blitz Program, review the agenda, conduct the *Cold Calling Techniques (That Really Work!)* quiz, and assess call scripts:

Introduction of Blitz Program – explain the purpose of the program

To gain new opportunities through outbound prospecting calls by scheduling appointments with qualified prospects or by generating qualified leads.

Review of The Prospecting Blitz Agenda (Appendix D)

Review the agenda and field questions about the schedule and tasks.

Review Prize Flyer (Appendix D)

Explain to Blitz participants what prizes they are eligible to win by reviewing the printed prize flyer with them (Appendix D). Throughout the day participants will have the opportunity to win prizes based on their scheduled appointments or qualified leads. With each appointment scheduled, reps will blow their horn and write on an index card the following information regarding the prospect they've called:

- CONTACT NAME, COMPANY & PHONE NUMBER
- APPOINTMENT DATE & TIME
- OPPORTUNITY (what they plan on selling to the prospect during the appointment)

Index cards are then put in the big red bowl for the hourly drawing. The group is gathered each hour (note "prize drawing" in agenda) to determine the winner for the hour. The Blitz facilitator draws an index card from the bowl and then announces the winner. The winner is given one of the $15 prizes and then asked to share with the group information about the prospect, the opportunity, and what they said to get the appointment. Participants then go back to their desks to continue their outbound calls. The more appointments, and therefore entries, each representative gets, the better their chances to win.

Conduct Oral Cold Calling Quiz (Appendix F)

Throw candy (chocolate works best!) to those with right answers. Sound corny? Well, it is...but it WORKS to get everyone motivated and in the spirit.

Review Scripts

Ask for volunteers to share the scripts they've brought to make their calls. The group may decide on a standard script to use if there is one that everyone likes.

Rules of Engagement

Explain to participants they are to *focus solely on prospecting calls during the Blitz*. No e-mail, no work on proposals or other work, no talking to others, etc. There will be time for a break to get caught up on other work, after lunch, before the second half of the Blitz. Also, remind them that for every appointment they set or lead they generate, they must blow their horn and enter their index card for a prize.

Finally, explain the *Blitz Numbers Tracking Worksheet* (Appendix E). At the end of the day the person with the most appointments or qualified leads is awarded the grand prize valued at $100 (cash works best!).

The Crying Towel

If you purchased Sittig Northwest's The Prospecting Blitz Kit on www.sittignw.com then pull out "The Crying Towel." Explain that the person who does not focus or is distracted and not fully participating in the Blitz, will receive the "crying towel." Read some of the "excuses" to the group and have fun with this throughout the day when walking around and evaluating the sales reps as they make their calls.

Some example "crying towel" lines include:

- My Quota is too high!
- My Territory is too big!
- My Territory is too small!
- We keep missing each other!
- I didn't want to appear overly anxious, so I thought I'd wait!
- My dog ate my leads!
- I sent them information!
- Quota…What Quota?
- The economy is bad!

Say to someone who isn't paying attention or who isn't focused, "Are you going to be the one who gets the crying towel?"

Open up to Q&A before starting calls

STEP 4: Start the Prospecting Blitz
Begin Calls

In this step, each person goes to his/her own desk to make his or her calls. The focus is to schedule appointments and generate leads, not to sell anything over the phone (unless that's the typical way your reps sell, then it's okay to sell over the phone). As the Blitz facilitator, walk around and evaluate reps as they are making their calls. Sit with them and listen to them. During the hourly prize drawing, mention to the group a couple of people who are doing well on the phone or who are scheduling a lot of appointments. Have those reps share what they are saying to get the appointments and generate leads with the rest of the group. Remind reps during calls not to do any other work, to blow their horn with each scheduled appointment, complete one index card for each appointment or lead, and to tally their results on the *Blitz Numbers Tracking Worksheet* (Appendix E) as they go. Call Blitz periods should be in one hour increments, meeting in the conference room to award the hourly prize drawing after each hour of calls. The hourly prize award and discussion should not be longer than fifteen minutes.

Results Tally

Also, on a white board that everyone can see, track results throughout the day by writing each rep's name and then a tick mark next to their name for each appointment scheduled. That way everyone can see who is on track to win the Grand Prize!

Lunch Break

Review the morning calls and discuss results tally on white board so far. Share successes and frustrations and discuss what's working and what's not working. Discuss common objections and how to overcome them. Refer to the cold calling book if necessary. The chapter on *the ledge* is great for overcoming objections. Give the reps about a thirty minute break after lunch to attend to other work, return voicemail, e-mail, etc.

Back to the Phones

After lunch reps are on the phone again for two hours, with a prize-drawing break in between in the conference room, just like with the morning calls. Refer to the agenda, if necessary, to get the reps back on track for the afternoon.

STEP 4: Wrap It Up

The final gathering in the conference room after the last hour of calls will consist of the final hourly prize drawing, reviewing the results tally from the group, and awarding the grand prize, as well as recording each rep's individual numbers based on their *Blitz Numbers Tracking Worksheet* (Appendix E) results worksheet tally.

Build an Excel spreadsheet with all of the appointments and/or opportunities scheduled for each rep and track them as they close to understand the return on investment value of your Blitz.
Finally, schedule your next Blitz!

Customized Blitz Options

Customized, professionally facilitated Blitz programs are available through Sittig Northwest, Inc. and include:

- All items associated with the Blitz (candy, horns, books, quiz, prizes, *Blitz Numbers Tracking Worksheets*, etc.)
- Video clip during the morning session relating to sales
- Prospecting Skills Training during morning and lunch sessions
- Customized flashcards to assist in overcoming common objections
- Results reports

Contact Sittig Northwest, Inc. today to schedule your customized Blitz at 206.769.4886 or info@sittignw.com.

13

Winning Ambassadors

What is an ambassador? An ambassador is the best networking partner you'll ever find, and the fastest way to bring your product or service to market. Having an ambassador is like having a salesperson who works just for you. Specifically, an ambassador is someone outside your organization, preferably inside an organization that is a client or who you would like to have as a client, who believes wholeheartedly in you and the product or service you sell. So much so that as your ambassador he is willing to *sell* your product or service among his peers and colleagues as well as within his own organization. Winning ambassadors requires that your product or service contain three main criteria. First, it's not enough anymore to simply *save* a client time and money; you must now be able to show that what you offer will actually *make* your client money, actually increase their revenue, and improve their bottom line. Keep in mind, there are creative ways of showing this if what you sell can't show in hard dollars but will improve your client's bottom line. For example, if you are a printing company, it's pretty tough to show that printing business cards, brochures, and other marketing collateral will make money for your client. But, what if the quality of work you do is so much better than that of your competition that you can show your print job will get noticed, more than that of your competition? What if your print job presents a better image for your client than the competition's print job? What if you are able to make recommendations to your client, based on their specific requirements, as to the appropriate paper, ink, formatting, etc., so that the marketing collateral you print for them is exactly the image they want to portray? Then couldn't you argue that by allowing your client to present a better image up front, based on the quality of work you provide, your client is more likely to get that extra deal or two a year? What is an extra deal or two a year worth, in terms of hard dollars, to your client?

The reason I use this as an example is because I was a client of a local printing company who I found out later, did *not* make the right recommendations to me in terms of ink, paper, and formatting. As such, I found out about a year later that the brochure I had been sending in the mail was completely smeared with ink and actually looked dirty by the time my prospect received it! It was only when I was considering using a new printing company for a new brochure that I discovered this. The new printer asked to see copies of my old brochure so he would have a feel for the type of paper, ink, etc. my project would require so I mailed him an old brochure. When we met in person to go over my options for the new brochure, he showed me the old brochure I had sent him in the mail. I was horrified to think I'd been sending that brochure in the mail for the past year to so many prospects! The inside of the brochure was black and red ink printed on glossy white paper. Because of the paper and ink combination my previous printer used, the black and red ink had smeared all over the white glossy paper. The ink was dry, but due to the movement of the brochure pages against each other within the envelope, the ink had created smudges all over the inside of the brochure. Needless to say, I never used my previous printing company again. The new printing company I began working with won my current and all of my future business based on his recommendations of how to improve the smeared ink problem by using a heavier, better quality paper and a different type of ink that would not smear. Now, I actually receive compliments on my new brochures not only for the design, but for the quality of the paper and crispness of the ink. I'm convinced that I will earn that extra deal or two a year based on the first impression that I am now presenting when I send out a new brochure as my first point of contact with a new prospect. An extra deal or two a year could be worth tens of thousands of dollars to me, so I conclude that by using this new printing company, I am actually making more money now than I was when I used my old printing company!

The second ambassador winning criterion is that your product or service needs to make your ambassador look good to his peers. In other words, the ambassador needs to feel proud that he discovered you, like you are a golden nugget or little known treasure that only your ambassador found.

Meeting this criterion requires that you provide the very best quality product or service in a timely manner, at a reasonable price. (I will cover selling on value and investment versus selling on cost and price in another chapter later in this book.) You must under-promise and over-deliver in every case when dealing with your ambassador and his company. From meeting your ambassador's colleagues for the first time, to managing the project, including offering client service and invoicing, you must consistently provide the best quality work available anywhere in your industry. Finally, if your ambassador prefers it, keep him apprised of your dealings with his company. Your ambassador may or may not want you to do this, so just ask and he will let you know.

I have several ambassadors that consistently sell my program to their peers, colleagues, and channel partners. One of them is a marketing firm that actually builds my program into the marketing plans she provides for her clients. Another ambassador, who is the president of a commercial furniture manufacturing rep firm, asked me to create a PowerPoint presentation for him to present to his industry manufacturing companies and dealer network in an effort to sell my programs! Finally, my most well-known ambassador, a software manufacturing company, sells my programs to their OEM (Original Equipment Manufacturers) network. Without exception, I've shown each of my ambassadors how my offering will make them money and make them look good. I also keep them apprised of my dealings with those they have recommended to me. Now that this ambassador network has been established, it continues to grow exponentially and I find myself doing less marketing and more delivering of my programs, resulting in the hiring of two new employees to meet the demand my ambassador network has created. My company has become more profitable because I am spending less time and energy marketing my programs and looking for new clients and more time doing the work I get paid for, which is implementing my programs!

Ambassadors are the cheapest sales team you will ever find. You don't have to pay them a salary. You don't even have to pay them a commission or bonus and you don't have to offer any extravagant incentives, although it is nice to appreciate your ambassadors as much as you can by taking them to lunch every now and then and remembering them during the holidays! This model of going to market is extremely effective and valuable when you consider the time and money you will save in finding new clients. Just find a few ambassadors and let them seek and find your new clients for you!

ACTIVITY: Define Ambassador Prospects

An *Ambassador Prospect* is defined as someone in your current customer database who works for a company that has the potential to increase its business with your company. Review your current customer database and choose two or three *Ambassador Prospects*. Nurture those *Ambassador Prospect* relationships and develop them into true *Ambassadors* for you and your company.

14

Planning and Facilitating Workshops

orkshops can help you:

- Create interest for your products and services with suspects and prospects
- Convert suspects into prospects
- Showcase your best customers and the results you've created for them to win new customers
- Fill your pipeline with new, qualified opportunities
- Make prospecting fun—workshops can be the most powerful prospecting tool of all!

Some of my best customers have come out of the prospecting workshops I facilitate about once a quarter.

The first thing to consider when planning a workshop is what prospects will get out of it. You may want to consider providing some value added content and not just a sales pitch; however, as long as the appropriate expectation is set with those you invite, a straight sales pitch workshop can be very effective. You can easily position what participants will get out of your workshop as an *opportunity to learn more about your products and services.*

There are two things you can do to create a draw to your workshop. First, choose a venue that is appealing. For example, I am a member of The Columbia Tower Club, a business club that sits on the 75th floor of the Bank of America building, the tallest skyscraper in Seattle. It is a beautiful club with amazing views of the city, delicious food, and outstanding service.

It is somewhat known by people in the business community in Seattle and those who are not members are often curious about what it has to offer. I reserve a private room at the club that seats about fifteen people comfortably, provide a continental breakfast, and validate parking for my guests. Because it is not cheap, I only invite those suspects I'm confident I can convert into prospects, who I know I will likely convert into customers. My prospecting workshops are not open to the general public and are available only to those who are invited. This positions the workshops as special and exclusive events with those who are invited.

Next, sending out invitations in the mail (not e-mail) can also be an effective way to get people to attend. People are so bombarded with e-mail these days that they may not even see an invitation that is sent electronically, or it may be filtered out due to spam software many companies are now utilizing. By sending an invitation in the mail, you accomplish a couple of things. First, it is more likely your invitation will be read by the person you've sent it to, especially if it looks like an invitation, because, let's face it, we all like to be invited to things. And secondly, it's a nice touch and shows that you've taken the time to think specifically of that person you are inviting, which sets a more personal tone. The other important element to the invitations is to *handwrite* the contact name and mailing address. People are much more likely to open the handwritten envelopes first, before any other mail.

Once the workshop has begun, there are a couple of ways to establish credibility with the audience, i.e. your suspects. First, have someone introduce the presenter, rather than for the presenter to introduce himself; however, the presenter should write the introduction. By having someone else introduce the presenter, you accomplish two things. One, the person making the introduction can rave about the presenter and speak to all his accomplishments, awards, and accolades. If the presenter himself speaks to his own accomplishments, awards, and accolades, it may sound arrogant or boastful. Two, by having the presenter introduced by someone else, it positions him (the presenter) as the expert.

The second thing you can do to establish credibility with participants is to have one of your best current customers sit in at your workshop and at some point offer a testimonial about the results you have created for them.

I always do this, inviting a different customer each time. During the presentation, it works beautifully to ask your current customer about their experience in working with you and your company. Obviously, letting your customer know ahead of time you're going to do this is a good idea. Talk with your customer about what the purpose of the workshop is and what you would like their role to be during the workshop. Ask your customer, before inviting them to the workshop, what their experience has been in working with you and your company so you know it's a good experience before including them in the workshop.

Establishing credibility with the audience—in this case, suspects for your products and services—is important to retain their attention throughout the presentation so that you have a chance to convert them into prospects later.

As I mentioned previously, consider offering something as a part of your workshop that is considered a value-add by your audience. Whether the value be in the content you deliver, or some other attribute of the workshop, something that is perceived by your suspects as additional value in attending your workshop will not only get them there, but increase your chances of converting them from suspects to prospects. For example, the value-add for the suspects I invite to my workshops is the natural networking that takes place before and after the pitch. I encourage networking by having everyone introduce themselves and share a little bit about what they do. When the people at the workshop connect with each other, I leverage that in my follow-up with each suspect.

And finally, if you're going for the hard close, during the workshop you can even offer a special workshop promotion with exclusive pricing and a set deadline when the promotion will expire. This also gives you a reason to follow up with the participants in your workshop to find out if they want to take advantage of the special promotion.

ACTIVITY PART ONE: Choose a Topic and Venue for Your Workshop

ACTIVITY PART TWO: Create a List of Prospects to Invite (Include One Client as a Sit-In Testimonial)

Part Three: Creating Powerful Proposals

15

Writing the Proposal

P roposals can make or break any sales deal and a well-written proposal can help cinch the deal. The proposal is your opportunity to show that you truly understand your prospect's needs, that you have listened to them intently, and that you have a solution in mind. Think of your proposal as a sales tool. It is your final chance before asking for the order to make an impression on your prospect, so you want to be sure it's a good one.

There are ten key elements to writing a powerful proposal that will not only help you make a good final impression before closing the deal, but will actually help improve your close ratio.

First I will list the ten key elements, and then I will describe each one in detail. Finally I will provide an example of a proposal I use that is often the tool in my sales toolbox that cinches the deal.

The ten key elements to writing any powerful proposal are:
- Header Testimonial
- Opening Statement
- Scope of Work Statement
- Scope of Work Detailed Description
- Project Deliverables Description
- Pricing Information/Investment Details Description
- Return-on-Investment Statement
- Call to Action Statement

- Thank you Statement
- Footer Testimonial

The *header testimonial* is a quote from an existing client who has used your products and services in the same manner that you are now proposing to your prospect. The quote should include a statement that speaks to the results your solution has provided as well as statistics to back it up. Keep the quote short and to the point—not more than one or two sentences. The function of the header testimonial is to grab the attention of your prospect so he will keep reading the rest of your proposal, and not just skip to the pricing/investment section, which prospects often tend to do.

The next key element is the *opening statement.* The opening statement should include thanking your prospect for the opportunity to present your proposal, as well as an enthusiastic statement from you regarding your interest in providing a solution that will meet the needs of the prospect.

The third key element is the *scope of work statement,* a one or two sentence description of your understanding of the prospect's needs, and the solution you are proposing to address those needs.

Next, the *scope of work detailed description* is the place where you provide details of the project, including the solution itself, and any relevant scheduling details including time frames and/or deadlines. It is also the portion of the proposal that speaks to items the prospect will be responsible for, if any, to make the project a success. It is important to set expectations of your prospect early so that they know exactly what they are agreeing to up front, before you close the deal.

The *project deliverables description*, the fifth element in writing a powerful proposal, includes the *tangible items* you will deliver as a part of your solution. The best way to present this portion of the proposal is to use bullet points to present clear concise action items associated with your solution.

The *pricing information/investment details description* is fairly self-explanatory; however, there are a few key points to consider when writing this section. First, while I refer to it here as *pricing information/investment details description,* in your proposal it should only be referred to as the *investment details* section. Stay away from words such as *cost* or *price*, and use the word *investment* instead. While *cost* and *price* indicate payment for something that doesn't necessarily have a return, the word *investment* indicates an asset or something valuable in exchange for payment. You want your prospect to feel that his payment for your solution is an *investment,* meaning he will get something valuable back. It is also important to put a deadline on your investment information to create a sense of urgency with the prospect and insure that the prospect moves through the sales process in a timely manner.

Essential for any proposal, but often missed, is the *return-on-investment statement.* Prospects want to know how and when they will see a *return* on the budget they've allocated for your project. Sometimes this requires some creativity on your part, and maybe you have to show the return in "soft dollars" (i.e. time savings or increased efficiency). If you are able to show a hard dollar return, based on average results experienced by previous and current clients, use it; it is by far the most compelling.

Next, the *call to action statement* asks your prospect to take some type of action to move forward in the sales process, such as signing the Agreement and assigning a purchase order number, if that is what's required of your prospects to place an order for your products or services. As mentioned before, be sure the call to action includes a deadline so your prospect knows *when* to sign and send the Agreement and purchase order number. Also, another wording tip: refer to your contract as an *Agreement*, not as a *contract. Agreement* suggests mutual acceptance of the solution you are proposing, while *contract* implies a scary, no-way-out commitment. While the difference in choosing one word over another may seem trivial, words do often stir emotions and you want your words to stir positive emotions to encourage your prospect to become your next customer.

Element number nine is the *thank-you statement.* You can never say thank you too many times throughout the sales process. You want your prospect to feel that you are interested and excited about the opportunity to work with him or her. This is your last chance in the proposal to show your enthusiasm for the project.

Finally, the *footer testimonial*, element number ten, is a testimonial or direct quote from a current customer that speaks to the satisfaction of the results you have created, that might also be created for the prospect you are currently proposing.

Now, let's bring it all together. Below I have provided an example of what a powerful proposal should look like, incorporating the ten elements previously discussed.

1)   HEADER TESTIMONIAL

"I really liked being a part of The Blitz Experience™. I and others could really see the energy in the air. In just one day, we had great success: 651 calls, 120 quotes and 40 sales, that's DOUBLE our typical daily production…WOW!!!!!!" Manager, Insurance Company

April 1, 2005

Bob Jones
ABC Company
1234 Main Street
Seattle, WA 98101

Dear Bob,

2)   OPENING STATEMENT

Thank you for the opportunity to submit a customized ***ABC Company Behavior Changing Blitz Experience™*** proposal. I am pleased to offer my expertise in the interactive sales training arena and look forward to a successful Blitz campaign!

3)   SCOPE OF WORK STATEMENT

Scope of Work
Based on our conversation and my understanding of the work involved in your project, Sittig Northwest will complete the following:

Creation, pre-planning, facilitation and implementation of a **Behavior Changing Blitz Experience™ Campaign**, which includes three phases.

4)   SCOPE OF WORK DETAILED DESCRIPTION

Curriculum

The Blitz training portion consists of learning the following techniques and practicing them on real customers and prospects focusing on outbound calls *during* the Blitz.

Getting past gatekeepers
Overcoming objections
Qualifying leads
Scheduling appointments
Leaving effective voice messages that get a response
Asking the right questions
Determining personal sales ratios to understand the required activity to reach sales goals
Moving forward in the sales process

5)   PROJECT DELIVERABLES DESCRIPTION

Project Deliverables

- Pre-Blitz assignment creation and distribution to all Blitz participants
- Three Phase Behavior Changing Blitz Experience™ Program facilitation for up to fifty sales reps per phase at ABC locations to include Fremont, CA, Lenexa, KS and Dallas, TX, including morning and mid-day training sessions, tally of ongoing results throughout the Blitz, break snacks, and Blitz results reports.
- All items associated with the Blitz Program are included: books, agenda, prize flyer, tips & tricks, index cards, horns, outbound call Blitz numbers tracking worksheets, overcoming objections flashcards, prizes, candy, snacks, video, "crying towel," and results reports.

6)   PRICING INFORMATION/INVESTMENT DETAILS DESCRIPTION

Investment Details
(*Must receive signed Agreement and payment by April 8, 2005 in order to properly prepare for the Behavior Changing Blitz Experience™ Program beginning May 16, 2005. Individual phase investment applies only with purchase of three phase program.)

Recommended Schedule for Blitz Program Phase One*	Total
Dallas Blitz Program May 17, 2005; 8a.m. – 4p.m.	$$$$$$$
Fremont Blitz Program May 19 & 20, 2005; 8a.m. – 4p.m.	$$$$$$$
Lenexa Blitz Program May 24, 2005; 8a.m. – 4p.m.	$$$$$$$
Investment* (includes all 3 locations of up to 50 salespeople total, + $$$ each additional salesperson over 50. Does not include travel related expenses.)	$$$$$$$$*

Recommended Schedule for Blitz Program Phase Two*	Total
Dallas Blitz Program July 12, 2005; 8a.m. – 4p.m.	$$$$$$$
Fremont Blitz Program July 14 & 15, 2005; 8am – 4pm	$$$$$$$
Lenexa Blitz Program July 22, 2005; 8a.m. – 4p.m.	$$$$$$$
Investment* (includes all 3 locations of up to 50 salespeople total, + $$$ each additional salesperson over 50. Does not include travel related expenses.)	$$$$$$$$

Recommended Schedule for Blitz Program Phase Three*	Total
Dallas Blitz Program September 6, 2005; 8a.m. – 4p.m.	$$$$$$$

Fremont Blitz Program September 8 & 9, 2005; 8a.m. – 4p.m.	$$$$$$$
Lenexa Blitz Program September 13, 2005; 8a.m. – 4p.m.	$$$$$$$
Investment* (includes all 3 locations of up to 50 salespeople total, + $$$ each additional salesperson over 50. Does not include travel related expenses.)	**$$$$$$$$$*** **Grand Total** **$$$$$$$$$***

7) RETURN-ON-INVESTMENT STATEMENT

If a new customer is worth $$$ and your average close ratio is 10% or better, based on average Blitz Experience™ results, you will make money as a result of this program.

8) CALL TO ACTION STATEMENT

If the above information matches your understanding of the project and meets your approval, please review and sign the attached Independent Contractor Agreement and mail, along with a 50% deposit payment of $$$$$$$ by April 8, 2005 to:

> Andrea Sittig-Rolf
> Sittig Northwest, Inc.
> P.O. Box 2423
> Redmond, WA 98073-2423

9) THANK YOU STATEMENT

Thank you for this fantastic opportunity, Bob. I am very excited about this project and look forward to working with you and ABC COMPANY!

Sincerely,
Andrea Sittig-Rolf
Andrea Sittig-Rolf
Blitz Master & CEO
Sittig Northwest, Inc.
www.sittignw.com
206-769-4886

10)   FOOTER TESTIMONIAL

"I had been leaving messages for months (with no returned calls) for the president of one of my reseller clients…Using a technique I learned during The Blitz Experience™, on a Friday afternoon I left a message for the president of the company…by noon on the following Monday he returned my call! The difference between this training program and others I have attended is that we <u>*applied*</u> *the techniques we learned the SAME DAY during the Blitz program." Sales Executive, Computer Company*

ACTIVITY: Write Your Next Proposal Using the Above Described Methodology

Part Four: Building Powerful Strategic Alliances
Establishing Win-Win Partnerships

16

Defining a Strategic Alliance

Webster's dictionary defines the word *strategy* as the science or art of military command as applied to the overall planning and conduct of large-scale combat operations. The word *alliance* is defined as a formal pact of confederation between nations in a common cause. Therefore, *a strategic alliance*, as it relates to business, might be defined as the science or art of sales tactics applied to the overall planning and conduct of large-scale business operations agreed to between companies with a common cause. And, as we all know, the common cause of most companies is to sell, sell, sell!

So, how can a strategic alliance help companies sell more? Think back to the time when you were little and you ran your very own lemonade stand. If you were like me, you sat out in front of your house with your best friend, a couple of TV trays, a pitcher of lemonade, and a stack of paper cups. Maybe you had a sign made out of cardboard: *Lemonade 10¢*. Then you'd just sit and wait for the customers to come pouring in, no pun intended, to buy your product. Just how effective was that strategy? What if, instead of sitting in front of your house to sell the lemonade, you convinced your parents to contact the mobile deli units that stop at construction sites at lunch time to sell food to the construction workers? Then, you sold your lemonade in larger quantities, at a discount of course, to the mobile deli unit owners to then turn around and sell your lemonade to the construction workers? What better audience for your product than a bunch of hot, sweaty, thirsty construction workers, and who else to get your product to them but the mobile deli units?

The most important thing to consider when forming a strategic alliance is that both parties need to benefit from it. In this case, you're selling lemonade in larger quantities and the mobile deli unit owners are able to offer fresh, homemade lemonade to their customers, and likely at a decent profit. Okay, so it's a little far fetched, I know, but you get my drift.

The point is that by aligning yourself with other companies who share a common goal and a common audience of prospects, you spend less effort prospecting and sell more of your products and services as a result. Let me give you another more realistic example.

Several years ago I worked as a regional sales manager for a data cabling company. We installed data cabling, i.e. wiring associated with connecting telephones and computers in an office setting. We were aligned with general contractors, electrical companies, and sometimes architects, because they often knew about projects we could participate in before we did. We rarely sold directly to the end user, but rather, through these alliances.

One alliance I established while working for this data cabling company was with a local business telephone systems company. The beauty of this alliance was that while the business telephone systems company sold telephone systems hardware, they did not do any wiring. They were completely dependent on outsourcing the wiring installation to independent contractors. I immediately realized a compelling partnership between the data cabling company I worked for at the time and the business telephone systems company. I approached my operations manager with the idea to form a strategic alliance with the business telephone systems company so that each time they sold a new phone system, they would contact us to install the wiring associated with it. The operations manager loved the idea, so next I approached the operations manager of the business telephone systems company. He also loved the idea because he was tired of dealing with the independent, often unreliable or unavailable independent contractor installers. This alliance was so successful my company had to hire a technician manager and six new technicians just to support this brand new line of business. We made millions of dollars in revenue from this alliance and the business telephone systems company now had a reliable and always available partner to install the wiring associated with their telephone systems; thus, creating a win-win partnership for us both.

Another more recent example is an alliance of my current company, Sittig Northwest, Inc., with a marketing firm called Go-To-Market Strategies, mentioned previously in this book. Go-To-Market Strategies often includes my sales training program, The Blitz Experience™, in their marketing proposals for their clients. Part of the service they offer to their clients is strategy around increasing sales, and The Blitz Experience™ is one tactical activity within the overall strategy for their clients to increase sales. By empowering Go-To-Market Strategies to include The Blitz Experience™ in their marketing proposals, I spend less effort prospecting and still sell more of my program than I would if I did not have this alliance. In return, Go-To-Market Strategies is able to offer an effective prospecting program to their clients, without actually having to deliver it, which is of great benefit to Go-To-Market Strategies.

17

Identifying Strategic Alliance Partners

The key to identifying strategic alliance partners is to determine their audience or sphere of influence. A *sphere of influence* is defined as *a territorial area over which political or economic influence is wielded by one nation.* For our purposes here, a *sphere of influence* might be defined as the audience, or prospects and customers, of the organization that you are considering for a strategic alliance. For a strategic alliance to be effective and work for both parties involved, both parties must share a common core audience of prospects and customers. Think of some common strategic alliances with whom most of us are familiar. Microsoft, for example, has many strategic alliances or partners, commonly known as OEMs (Original Equipment Manufacturers). Such OEMs include Dell, Hewlett Packard, and IBM. Microsoft doesn't sell directly to the end user, so they formed strategic alliances with companies who needed an operating system for the computers they manufacture. Both Microsoft and the OEMs have the same core audience of prospects and customers. They both get value from the partnership. Microsoft gets its products distributed through the OEMs and the OEMs get to use the power of the Microsoft brand to better position their products in the marketplace.

In my business, for example, it makes sense to form strategic alliances with sales and marketing strategy consulting firms who focus on the best sales strategy for their clients but don't actually deliver from a tactical standpoint. The Blitz Experience™ sales training program is a tactical piece that fits in nicely with an overall go-to-market or sales strategy. So, for instance, one of my partners is called Realized Performance, a high-end business consulting firm with sales and marketing strategy as one of its core competencies (www.realizedperformance.com). If they have a client who has a brand new product they want to introduce to the market, Realized Performance might include The Blitz Experience™ as a part of their overall strategy in promoting that particular product. Realized Performance does not have the staff or desire to implement all of the tactical pieces of their strategic recommendation, so they outsource some of the tactical pieces to their subcontractors and resource partners, such as my company, Sittig Northwest, Inc. Again, we both get value from the relationship. Not only is Realized Performance able to offer a full suite of strategy and tactics recommendation for their clients, without having to actually implement all of the tactical pieces, they also have a new profit center by utilizing Sittig Northwest, Inc. to implement the sales training tactics they recommend. Furthermore, Sittig Northwest doesn't have to spend as much time directly prospecting for new clients since the alliance with Realized Performance often provides that function of the sales process.

This concept as a prospecting strategy is very powerful, especially when it is duplicated by way of multiple strategic alliances. The more strategic alliances you have, the less direct prospecting you will need to do, as your strategic alliance partners take care of that function of the sales process for you. Imagine if instead of spending the majority of your day cold calling and asking for referrals, you handled incoming requests for your products and services from your strategic alliance partners? In effect, the strategic alliance partners are bringing your new clients to you.

While cold calling and referral marketing are also effective prospecting strategies, and may produce more immediate results, the strategic alliance prospecting strategy offers a continuing pipeline of new business development opportunities, once the alliance is established and running. The strategic alliance prospecting strategy will take longer to implement than many other common prospecting activities; however, it is by far the best long-term strategy for consistent business development.

ACTIVITY: Identify One Strategic Alliance Partner Prospect

18

Answering the Question:
What's in It for Them?

B y now you've probably noticed a common theme in this section about strategic alliances benefiting *both* parties involved. It is absolutely critical that before approaching a strategic alliance prospect, you determine what the value is for them in partnering with you. If you can show that they will make money as a result of an alliance with your company, it's pretty much a no-brainer and you will likely win them as a partner. If, however, the only value-add you bring is convenience or other "soft benefits," you will have a harder sell. Providing an additional profit center for the strategic alliance partner prospect you approach will get their attention immediately and give you the opportunity to explore a mutually beneficial partnership.

Get creative. As a part of the activity provided at the end of this chapter, write down a few ideas that speak to the ways in which your strategic alliance partner prospect will make money as a result of partnering with you. Think of all the things your company provides that they don't already have in place, or that they may have in place, but that your company can do a better job at providing. Consider how your products and services will benefit your strategic alliance partner's customers, and whether or not it makes sense for your strategic alliance partner prospect to offer your products and services to their customers.

When you are able to establish that your strategic alliance proposal will not only provide some soft benefits to your strategic alliance partner prospect but can also show how partnering will provide an additional profit center for them, then you have a compelling reason to approach and explain your partnership idea to your strategic alliance partner prospect.

ACTIVITY: Summarize the Benefits of Your Proposed Strategic Alliance to Your Strategic Alliance Partner Prospect

Part Five: Writing Compelling Case Studies

Leveraging Your Best Clients as Your Number One Sales Tool

19

Writing a Summarized Case Study

D o you have happy customers? You know, the ones who are loyal, think you're the greatest, and continue to buy from you time and time again? Why not leverage the relationships with those customers to gain *new* customers to further develop your business? Detailed accounts of your most satisfied clients are your best selling tool. When others have something positive to say about you and the products or services you provide, it establishes credibility with prospects who are considering buying what you sell. The case studies you write should be results oriented so they address what buyers care about most when considering a purchase—results. Here I will give examples of two different types of case studies. The first is an example of a summarized case study that is short and to the point, stating facts without much narrative description. The second is an example of a benefits-based, narrative-in-description case study. Here is the outline to follow for a *Summarized Case Study*:

Client:	Name of the client for this case study.
Challenge:	State the challenge that faced your client before you worked with them.
Solution:	Describe the solution you provided.
Result:	Describe the result based on the solution you provided.
Testimonial:	Include a quote from the client describing the result you provided.

Here is an example of a summarized case study I have used as a selling tool for The Blitz Experience™ sales training program:

Client: ABC Telecommunications Company

Challenge: Revenue was down with the company at 23% of its line
goal.* Sales reps were unmotivated and lacked the
consistency of the activity necessary for the company to
reach its revenue goals.

Solution: The Blitz Experience™ program including 3 sessions, 45
days apart.

Result: 91 appointments with new prospects, 35 new accounts and
105% of line goal.*

*"Since our Sittig Northwest Blitz Experience™ kick-off, our sales reps have changed
their behavior to consistent, proactive selling activities that have resulted in tremendous
revenue growth for our company. Thanks Sittig Northwest, we couldn't have done it
without you!"* VP Sales, ABC Telecommunications Company

(*Line goal is defined as the number of telephone lines sold with ABC
Telecommunications Company services attached such as long distance,
local service, DSL, and the like.)

20

Writing a Benefits-Based Case Study

T he second type of case study is called the *Benefits-based, Narrative-in-description Case Study*. Here is an outline to follow for this type of case study:

State a description of the client in terms of their industry, size, core competency and/or business purpose or mission.

Client:	Name of the client for this case study.
Challenge:	State the challenge in detail that faced your client before you worked with them, focusing on the business pain they were experiencing.
Solution:	Describe the solution you provided, focusing on the *benefits* of your solution versus any features associated with your solution.
Result:	Describe the result based on the solution you provided, focusing again on the *benefits* of the result.
Testimonial:	Include a quote from the client describing the result you provided.

Following is an example of this type of case study that I wrote *as a customer* of an audio and web-based conferencing company I will refer to as XYZ Conference Service.

> Sittig Northwest, Inc. is a results oriented, activity based sales training and new business development firm that helps companies increase sales through the creation and implementation of

effective Blitz Experience™, Team Building and Lead Generation Programs.

Challenge: Traditional means of presenting to prospects face-to-face in other states and countries was becoming so expensive and inefficient that I was considering limiting my prospecting efforts to my local area. I needed a solution that would allow me to fully present my sales training programs through both a visual and an audio process in an effort to fully engage my prospects. I was concerned about the ease-of-use of a high-tech solution for both my prospects as the participants and myself as the presenter. I was also concerned my prospects might find a Web-based method of presenting my sales training solutions as being unfriendly or impersonal.

Solution: XYZ Conference Service offered not only a user-friendly audio and Web-based visual conferencing solution for Sittig Northwest and my prospects, but stayed hands on with me as the conference call facilitator until I was completely comfortable using the service. XYZ's responsiveness to my questions was immediate and their willingness to help me with trial runs the day before a conference call was incredibly helpful.

Result: Sittig Northwest has become much more efficient both in the time and expenses associated with presenting sales training programs to prospects in other states and countries, and as a result, I have closed more business! The XYZ Web-based conference solution has been very well received by prospects as it is both easy to use and offers them the convenience of participating in the conference call from their own home or office. Sittig Northwest is no longer limited to prospecting in my local area. Because of the XYZ solution, I no longer have boundaries and can literally prospect all over the world!

Testimonial: *"XYZ Conference Service has provided Sittig Northwest, Inc. with an invaluable tool that allows unlimited prospecting capabilities. As a result, I have increased my business and my bottom line! I experienced an instant return on investment by using XYZ to develop new business with companies outside my local area."*
Andrea Sittig-Rolf, President & CEO, Sittig Northwest, Inc.

Don't be afraid to ask for testimonials. When you've done a good job in working with a client, ask for their permission to either include them as a case study in your case study portfolio, or to give a testimonial regarding the work you've done. Often, clients are more agreeable if you make it as easy for them as possible.

For example, you should be the one to write the case study or testimonial and just ask your client to give you his permission to use it. Not only does this save your client time, it allows you to convey the message you want to convey and to best profile the work you've done for that particular client. It also guarantees a faster turnaround of the case study since you're not waiting on your customer to finish it.

If you have a storefront or office where clients and prospects visit frequently, framing actual testimonial letters on client letterhead with the client's signature can be a very effective way to get your message across and gain instant credibility with your prospects. If you do not have a storefront or office where clients and prospects visit frequently, it is also just as effective to use case studies as a part of your Web site in a "case studies" category or within a presentation, such as PowerPoint, or in other marketing materials such as brochures or direct mail pieces. Case studies are the most cost-effective sales tool there is and if nothing else, you can print them on company letterhead to share with prospects.

Case studies are also wonderful for overcoming objections. For example, when you hear the objection, "I'm not interested," you can refer to a case study of a client with a similar objection who has since used your products or services with great results.

It is a good idea to categorize case studies by industry, company size, and application of your products or services. When prospecting, you can then refer to the case study that best fits the prospect you are working with. So, for example, if you are working with a small, telecommunications company who will use your widget to make their billing process more efficient, share with them a case study that profiles a small, telecommunications company who used your widget to make their billing process more efficient. This becomes extremely valuable to your prospect by giving them confidence that you can produce the results they desire.

I have twenty-four case studies, each profiling a different Sittig Northwest offering, for different sized companies in a variety of industries who used my services in a specific way to help them increase their sales and make their salespeople more effective. By writing a compelling case study for each happy client, I have created a virtual library of case studies—an invaluable resource used to continue to grow my customer base.

Case studies should be used throughout the sales process from introducing your products or services to including them in proposals, overcoming objections, and finally asking for the order. Because case studies highlight the *results* your company has been able to create for your customers, they keep your results top of mind with your prospects. I can almost guarantee that your competitors are not doing this, so all other things being equal, you will gain the competitive advantage by providing for your prospects what your competitors do not!

A great way to gain the information you'll need for your case studies is to provide an evaluation form to each client upon completion of their project. Be sure to ask open-ended questions in your evaluations so that your clients are giving you the details of their experience in their own words. This is also your opportunity to ask for referrals so be sure to include a question in your evaluation that asks for referrals.

The evaluation you provide will actually accomplish a couple of different things. First, it will show your new client that their feedback is important to you and that you value their opinion and their business. Then, it will give you the information you need for your case study regarding their particular project. Finally, it will give you the opportunity to become a hero and fix anything that went wrong during the process of working with your client.

Below I have provided a copy of the evaluation form I use at the completion of a Blitz Experience™ project with a client. It demonstrates the use of open-ended questions such as questions that start with the words *who, what, why, where, when, and how,* and statements that begin with *please share, please describe or tell me about.*

Sittig Northwest Blitz Experience™ Program Evaluation

1) How did the Sittig Northwest Blitz Program you participated in provide value in the development and implementation of new prospecting techniques?

2) What specific new selling techniques did you learn during the course of the Sittig Northwest Blitz Experience™ Program that you will continue to use as a part of your everyday prospecting activities?

3) What did you enjoy most about the Sittig Northwest Blitz Experience™ Program?

4) Please share any specific conversations you had that resulted in an appointment based on your use of the techniques you learned during the Blitz, keeping in mind the techniques we discussed pertaining to getting a voicemail returned, or your ability to overcome objections and then get the appointment.

5) What recommendations do you have that would improve the Sittig Northwest Blitz Program for future participants?

6) How often would you like to participate in a Sittig Northwest Blitz Program? (Please mark your choice with an "x".)

    a)   once a month _____

    b)   once a quarter _____

    c)   twice a year _____

    d)   once a year _____

    e)   never_____

7) What other companies do you know of that you would recommend should participate in this program? Please provide their contact information below. *(See how I am?! Asking for referrals!?!? Shameless I tell you, shameless!)*

_____

_____

_____

8) What other types of "follow up" programs, focusing on which specific selling techniques, would be useful to you?

9) Please use this space for any additional comments you have regarding the Sittig Northwest Blitz Experience™ Program.

Thank you for your participation!

ACTIVITY PART ONE: Write a Summarized Case Study

Write a *Summarized Case Study* based on one of your top clients following this simple formula:

Client: Name of the client for this case study.

Challenge: State the challenge that faced your client
                  before you worked with them.

Solution: Describe the solution you provided.

Result: Describe the result based on the solution you
                  provided.

Testimonial: Include a quote from the client describing the
                  result you provided.

ACTIVITY PART TWO: Write a Benefits-Based Case Study

Write a *Benefits-Based Case Study* based on another one of your top clients. Remember, this type of case study is more narrative in nature than the *Summarized Case Study,* therefore, follow this formula:

State a description of the client in terms of their industry, size, core competency, and/or business purpose or mission.

Client: Name of the client for this case study.

Challenge: State the challenge in detail that faced your client before
                  you worked with them, focusing on the business pain they
                  were experiencing.

Solution: Describe the solution you provided, focusing on the *benefits*
                  of your solution versus any features associated with your
                  solution.

Result: Describe the result based on the solution you provided,
                  focusing again on the *benefits* of the result.

Testimonial: Include a quote from the client describing the
                  result you provided.

Appendix A: Creative Strategies to Get a Response

I've practiced several effective strategies over the years that always get a response from prospects.

First, send mail, unfolded, in a 9X12 brightly colored envelope that matches your company colors. Handwrite the name and address of your prospect on a company mailing label that includes your logo, and place in the center of the envelope. Be sure to include enough postage as the larger envelopes require more postage than the standard size envelopes.

Next, *handwrite* a message on the back flap of the envelope to get the prospect's attention, such as, "Referred by *(referral source)*," "Information you requested enclosed," "Information as promised," or "Looking forward to meeting you." Anything you can write on the back flap of the envelope that creates curiosity will inspire the prospect to actually open and read your materials.

Mail something bulky. For example, mail one baby shoe with a note that says, "Just wanted to get my foot in the door." Or something else that relates to your business. For example, I often mail a kazoo to prospects. One, it's a prop I use in my sales training programs so it's directly relevant to my business; two, it's bulky so it creates curiosity; and three, it immediately sends a message that my program is *fun*, an important part of my brand that is easily conveyed using this technique. Be sure to include a return address on the outside of the envelope so it's sure to be delivered by the post office.

Get the prospect's attention by sending the "Skeleton Mailer," to be used only as a last resort! When a prospect you have been trying to reach has not responded to your many voice messages, send a rubber skeleton in a 9X12 brightly colored envelope that matches your company colors (as mentioned in #1 of this Appendix). Attach a business card to the toe of the skeleton by punching a hole in the business card and tying it on the skeleton's toe with a short ribbon. On the back of the business card write, "This is me, waiting for you, to call me back." Most people who have a sense of humor will respond to this, although you must choose carefully which prospects to send it to, based on the rapport you have with the prospect. (Rubber or plastic skeletons are carried by most novelty shops.)

The last strategy to get a response is to mail items that are tactile in nature; in other words, something to feel and interact with, again using something that relates to your business. Again, the kazoo in my business works great, so think about something tactical that relates to your business that you could mail.

Appendix B: The Top Three Indicators a Prospect is No Longer a Prospect

Indicator Final Attempt

1) You have left more than three e-mails or voicemails and the prospect has not responded.

Skeleton mailer as described in Appendix B, item # 4.

2) The prospect has promised to have an answer for you by a certain date and then pushes the date back more than three times, without a reasonable explanation.

Be direct in asking the prospect why the time line keeps changing. Ask whether or not it still makes sense for you to do business.
You might even say something like, "Does the original solution we've proposed still make sense or has something changed within your business that may require a revised proposal from us? If we provide a revised proposal addressing your new needs, when would you like to begin the project?"

3) The prospect has told you he's not interested now, never will be, and has asked you to stop calling!

NOTHING, You're done!

Appendix C: Ten Tactical Tips

1) Send a handwritten thank-you note after each meeting or other significant interaction with your prospects. Handwritten notes are great for any occasion or no occasion at all. If you send notes on a regular basis, you will be remembered. Also, people tend to hold on to handwritten notes which works well from a branding standpoint as well. Today people are so bombarded with e-mail that receiving a handwritten note is unique and often the first thing opened in the pile of mail sitting on your prospect's desk.

2) Mail newspaper or magazine articles to your prospects that relate to *their* business or hobbies, including articles that both relate and don't relate to your business.

3) Make good eye contact and offer a firm handshake to inspire confidence in you from the people you meet. I often say the name of the person when I am meeting them for the first time. For example, if Joe introduces himself to me, when making eye contact and shaking his hand, I say "Nice to meet you, Joe." This helps me remember his name and it's more personal than just saying, "Nice to meet you," without using his name.

4) Focus on building relationships with prospects, rather than on selling them. Some of my closest personal friends are a result of practicing this very methodology. And, of course, the side benefit is often that these prospects/friends will also become great customers.

5) Always do what you say you will do. During the sales process, this is a very important way to build credibility and create trust with your prospect. It shows the prospect that if during the sales process you follow through with your promises and commitments, that when your prospect becomes a customer, you will continue to do so.

6) Use the right words when working with prospects. For example, call your contract "paperwork" or an "agreement." Instead of saying the word "sign" when referring to signing the contract, say "authorize" or

"okay." Think of the scary words your prospects hear you say during the course of the sales process and try using different, less threatening words. Use your thesaurus if you have to. Tom Hopkins was the first one I heard using this technique years ago. It worked like a charm then, and it still does today.

7) Take some time each week to plan the following week. Often we end up in a reactive mode rather than proactive mode when managing our time, which puts us at a disadvantage. Schedule time in your calendar each week when you won't be interrupted to plan and also to review your goals from the following week. Plan your cold calls. Plan your meetings. Plan to plan. There is a famous quote I love: "If you fail to plan, you plan to fail," and it couldn't be more true.

8) Ask for help. One of the most powerful tools you have is the people you know who know what you don't know! Why reinvent the wheel when you can easily learn from others who have been there before you? When you empower others to help you in areas you are weak, it allows you to focus on your strengths, which is where you are more likely to enjoy success.

9) Contact your local business newspaper and find out how to submit an article you can write as an expert in your field. Most newspapers are open to such requests, and in fact, have a process for it already in place. To submit articles for consideration for publication, it usually requires that you sign your rights to the material over to the paper so they own the copyright. When you write an article about whatever it is you do, you are seen in the eyes of the readers not just as a salesperson, but as an expert. Be sure to include your contact information at the end of the article so readers know how to reach you.

10) Having a good sense of humor is essential when you choose sales as a profession, so use it to your advantage. Most people have and appreciate a good sense of humor and it is a great way to break the ice with new prospects, build relationships, and ultimately close sales. Having a

good sense of humor also shows a certain level of confidence which inspires confidence others have in you and helps build trust. It's true that people buy from people they like, and having a good sense of humor, confidence, and being trustworthy are all likable qualities.

Appendix D: Blitz Agenda and Prize Flyer

The Prospecting Blitz Agenda & Prize Template

Prizes	Agenda	
Starbucks Gift Card	8:30 a.m.:	Pre-Blitz Meeting & Quiz
	10:00 a.m.:	Calls begin
Borders Books Gift Card	11:00 a.m.:	Prize Drawing
	11:15 a.m.:	Calls continue
Closing Techniques **Book**	12:15 p.m.:	Prize Drawing
	12:30 p.m.:	Lunch / Q&A
Aroma Therapy Candles	1:30 p.m.:	Calls continue
	2:30 p.m.:	Prize Drawing
Grand Prize: $100!	2:45 p.m.:	Calls continue
	3:45 p.m.:	Prize Drawing Grand Prize Awarded Crying Towel Awarded
	4:00 p.m.:	Wrap Up

Appendix E: Blitz Numbers Tracking Worksheet (Please see the *Tracking Call Ratios* section in chapter 11 for a detailed explanation of this worksheet.)

Blitz Numbers Tracking Worksheet

CALLS	CONNECTS	APPOINTMENTS	CALL BACKS	NO's	PROPOSALS	SALES
OOOOO	OOOOO	OOOOO	OOOOO	OOOOO	OOOOO	
OOOOO	OOOOO	OOOOO	OOOOO	OOOOO		
OOOOO	OOOOO					
OOOOO	OOOOO					
OOOOO	OOOOO					
OOOOO	OOOOO	OOOOO	OOOOO	OOOOO	OOOOO	
OOOOO	OOOOO	OOOOO	OOOOO	OOOOO		
OOOOO	OOOOO					
OOOOO	OOOOO					
OOOOO	OOOOO					
OOOOO	OOOOO	OOOOO	OOOOO	OOOOO	OOOOO	
OOOOO	OOOOO	OOOOO	OOOOO	OOOOO		
OOOOO	OOOOO					
OOOOO	OOOOO					
OOOOO	OOOOO					
OOOOO	OOOOO	OOOOO	OOOOO	OOOOO	OOOOO	
OOOOO	OOOOO	OOOOO	OOOOO	OOOOO		
OOOOO	OOOOO					
OOOOO	OOOOO					
OOOOO	OOOOO					
TOTAL	TOTAL	TOTAL	TOTAL	TOTAL	TOTAL	$$ TOTAL $

Appendix F: Blitz Quiz
Cold Calling Techniques (That Really Work!) Quiz

What is the A-P-S formula? (**A**ppointments give you **P**rospects give you **S**ales)

Know your numbers (Reference *The Blitz Numbers Tracking Worksheet* – Appendix E) Review Chapter 2 together. Explain to participants that as they make their calls throughout the day, they will tally their results by filling in a bubble on the *Blitz Numbers Tracking Worksheet* each time they dial the phone, each time they connect with someone live, and each time they schedule an appointment, so by the end of the day, they will "know their numbers" and understand how many calls they need to make to schedule how many appointments. This can then be tracked further to include number of proposals and number of sales based on number of appointments and number of original phone calls.

What is a "no" quota? The number of "nos" it takes to get to a "yes."

What are 5 ways to potentially double your income? Double the number of calls, get through more often, get more appointments, close more sales, generate more dollars per sale. (Look at your personal numbers to discover what just one more contact a day will do for you.)

What is a "T" call? After an appointment, you go to the left and right of the building as well as across the street (or behind you) and come back to the office with three more contacts.

What are some other ways to generate leads? Civic or networking organizations, conferences, newspapers, existing business, directories, brokered lists, king county library, etc.

What are the five basic elements to the initial cold call? Get the person's attention, identify yourself and your company, give the reason for your call, make a qualifying question or statement, and set the appointment.

What is the reason for your call? To set the appointment only, not to sell your products or services.

What are the six tips for cold calling? Use a mirror to be sure you're smiling—vocal chords cannot be strained or sound tense when smiling, use a timer, practice, keep a record, tape record your calls, stand up.

What is the Ledge? Uses the first question or negative response as a foothold to turn an extended phone prospecting conversation around. Ledge examples in book, page 78 - 82

How can you leave a voicemail that will get a call back? Say you are calling about or in reference to ABC Company (a customer you have helped). Say you are calling about or in reference to "Bob Smith" ("Bob Smith", in this case, represents a salesperson who used to work at your company who is no longer there.)

Drill on overcoming common objections: *(Tip: Use a small nerf football with this exercise. As the Blitz Master, act as the customer giving an objection, throwing the ball to someone on the team, and then have them overcome the objection and throw the ball back to you.)*

Overcoming Common Objections

Common Objection Categories:

> **Not Interested (NI)** – You know, other companies we do business with told us exactly the same thing before they saw how what we offered could *benefit* them (in such and such a way).
> **Happy Now (HN)** – Other companies we do business with told us exactly the same thing before they saw how what we offered could *complement* what they were already doing.
> **Bad Experience** – Talk about how your company has *changed* since the bad experience.
> **Send Literature** – The Ledge: I'm just curious…ask a who, what, why, how question.

> I'm not interested. *(NI)*

I've already got it. *(HN)*

I have no time. *(NI)*

We just signed a contract yesterday. *(HN)*

We once had a problem with your company – *Bad Experience or (NI)*

I'm too busy to talk now. *(the only reason I'm calling is to set an appointment)*

We're happy now with what we've got, we're all set. *(HN)*

We don't need it. *(NI)*

I have no money. *(NI)* – *discuss affordable payment plans or other payment options*

We're working with your competition. *(HN)*

That's not a priority. *(NI)*

It just doesn't fit in. *(NI)*

We don't have the budget. *(NI)*

We don't do that. *(NI)*

We're all set. *(HN)*

How much is it? *The prices range from X to Y. I'm just curious, Ledge:* Can you send me some literature? *Can't we just get together? How's Tuesday at 3p.m.? Or of course, but I'm just curious, what are you doing right now … Of course, Ledge: but I'm just curious, how are you… (ask who, what, why, where, how questions) or say, Of course, but I just need a little more information so I can understand what information to send you…*

We hate you! *(NI)*

We have no reason to buy that right now. *(NI)*

We don't need anything else because we've already got exactly what you sell. *(HN)*

Before you go on, why should I switch to you? *Uniqueness of sales rep and what he brings to the table*

The president has decided against this. *(NI)*

What makes your company so good? *You do, there is no other you (you = sales rep)*

It's not in the plan. *(NI)*

Can you just give me the thirty second version of your presentation? *Ledge: Of course, but I'm just curious…ask an open-ended question*

We're doing it ourselves. *(HN)*

We're doing it in-house. *(HN)*

Appendix G: Keynotes, Workshops and Sales Training Programs Offered by Sittig Northwest, Inc.

Keynotes

Andrea Sittig-Rolf delivers informative and entertaining keynote speeches on sales-related topics at sales conferences and corporate events as well as association meetings. Choose from a variety of prepared keynotes, or have one customized especially for your event. Her animated and conversational style will engage your group immediately and will keep them learning and laughing throughout the presentation.

To learn more about the keynote offering, contact Sittig Northwest, Inc. at 206-769-4886, contactus@sittignw.com or visit www.sittignw.com.

Workshops

While Ms. Sittig-Rolf's keynotes address the *why,* her workshops address the *how.* Again, you may choose from a variety of prepared workshops on various sales-related topics, or have one customized for your group. Workbooks are provided and your team will walk away with some effective sales tools to implement on real prospects and customers long after the workshop is over.

To learn more about these workshops, contact Sittig Northwest, Inc. at 206-769-4886, contactus@sittignw.com or visit www.sittignw.com.

Sales Training Program

Sittig Northwest, Inc. is the developer and exclusive provider of an activity-based sales training program called The Blitz Experience™ that helps salespeople become more effective when prospecting over the phone. This unique sales training program requires prospecting activity the day of the training so that sales reps are actually filling their pipelines with new opportunities using the techniques taught *during* the training. The Blitz Experience™ clients have reported increased sales of as much as 20 percent as a direct result of this innovative sales training program.

To learn more about The Blitz Experience™, contact Sittig Northwest, Inc. at 206-769-4886, contactus@sittignw.com or visit www.sittignw.com.

About the Author

Andrea Sittig-Rolf helps sales organizations inspire change, maximize sales, and increase bottom line results. Business savvy with a passion for people, she understands how to help salespeople be their best and has what it takes to inspire them. Ms. Sittig-Rolf is a successful entrepreneur, author and sales trainer, and is in high demand as a speaker and workshop leader.

Ms. Sittig-Rolf has served on the board as president of The Business Network International, Seattle chapter, vice president of Programs for Sales and Marketing Executives International, Seattle chapter, as well as founded and served as president of The Alliance, a group of sales professionals who offered a B to B "one-stop shopping" service for their shared clients.

Ms. Sittig-Rolf is the creator of a column entitled "Sales Solutions" featured biweekly in The Puget Sound Business Journal, and contributor of 12 articles a month to SellingPower.com's One Minute Tip, featured daily on the SellingPower.com Web site.

Ms. Sittig-Rolf is also the founder and president of Sittig Northwest, Inc., a sales training and consulting organization based in Redmond, WA. She is the developer and exclusive provider of The Blitz Experience™, an activity-based sales training program designed to help salespeople become more effective when prospecting over the phone. Her sales training program is unique because it requires salespeople to practice what they learn the day of the training on real prospects resulting in new business opportunities at the end of the training.

Before starting Sittig Northwest, Inc. she held various sales-related positions, such as Senior Account Executive at Voice-Tel, Account Manager at Lucent Technologies, and Regional Sales Manager, President's Club, at ACS Dataline, where she consistently exceeded revenue goals.

Ms. Sittig-Rolf holds a B.A. in Psychology from Southwest Texas State University. She lives in Redmond, Washington with her husband, Brian.

Management
Best Sellers

Other Best Sellers

Visit Your Local Bookseller Today or www.Aspatore.com

for a Complete Title List

- How to Reduce IT Spending - Leading CTOs and Technology Executives on Specific Ways to Reduce Technology Expenses - $99.95
- Ninety-Six and Too Busy to Die - Life Beyond the Age of Dying - $24.95
- Technology Blueprints - Strategies for Optimizing and Aligning Technology Strategy & Business - $69.95
- The CEO's Guide to Information Availability - Why Keeping People & Information Connected is Every Leader's New Priority - $27.95
- Being There Without Going There - Managing Teams Across Time Zones, Locations and Corporate Boundaries - $24.95
- Profitable Customer Relationships - CEOs from Leading Software Companies on using Technology to Maximize Acquisition, Retention & Loyalty - $27.95
- The Entrepreneurial Problem Solver - Leading CEOs on How to Think Like an Entrepreneur and Solve Any Problem for Your Team/Company - $27.95
- The Philanthropic Executive - Establishing a Charitable Plan for Individuals & Businesses - $27.95
- The Golf Course Locator for Business Professionals - Organized by Closest to Largest 500 Companies, Cities & Airports - $12.95
- Living Longer Working Stronger - 7 Steps to Capitalizing on Better Health - $14.95
- Business Travel Bible - Must Have Phone Numbers, Business Resources, Maps & Emergency Info - $19.95

Call 1-866-Aspatore or Visit www.Aspatore.com to Order